Arrowheads & Projectile Points

Lar Hothem

COLLECTOR BOOKS
A Division of Schroeder Publishing Co., Inc.

The current values in this book should be used only as a guide. They are not intended to set prices, which vary from one section of the country to another. Auction prices as well as dealer prices vary greatly and are affected by condition as well as demand. Neither the Author nor the Publisher assumes responsibility for any losses that might be incurred as a result of consulting this guide.

Searching for a Publisher?

We are always looking for knowledgeable people considered to be experts within their fields. If you are that there is a real need for a book of your collectible subject and have a large comprehensive collection, contact Collector Books.

Additional copies of this book may be ordered from:

COLLECTOR BOOKS
P.O. Box 3009
Paducah, Kentucky 42002-3009

@ $7.95. Add $2.00 for postage and handling.

CONTENTS

Foreword

No other item crafted by prehistoric man has received such wide attention as have arrowheads and chipped projectile points. Collections, representing to the present generation finds of the earliest peoples, are abundant throughout North America. We are fortunate that such traces were left, for these and other chipped artifacts are frequently our only link to prehistoric man, clues to the habitation of North America. A collector's challenge is to bring the collection to life by searching for information and insight regarding projectile points.

The established writer on Amerind subjects and author of this book, Lar Hothem, has assembled a long-awaited classic reference on projectile points. An avid collector of such pieces, he has studied his subject in the field, museum and library. Only through thoroughness and persistence in tracking down sources of information, coupled with an ability to evaluate finds, can a writer proceed beyond an accumulation of facts to offer the reader new perspectives.

This books is an invitation to achieve a deeper appreciation of the subject, and it succeeds in presenting Indian points as artistic expressions of prehistoric man. This is a book of substance which no writer on the subject has previously dared attempt. It strikes a median between the collector and archaeologists, both amateur and professional.

Most readers will find the relative dollar figures valuable in assessing the quality of their points, in establishing trade worth, and in determining insurance coverage. Collectors and students, libraries and museums, will welcome the regional approach to projectile points.

Assembled within these pages is a near-complete reference on important aspects of point collecting, cataloguing, displaying, and identifying. Lar Hothem — recognizing that the appreciation of a collection is directly related to one's study and understanding of the subject — has shared his vast knowledge of the field.

Until now, no book attempted to reach (or teach) the basics of prehistoric points, how they were made, when and where, and by whom, and how collectors might consider all this. Thanks and congratulations to Lars Hothem for his successful resolve to bring us a fine reference.

John Barry
Davis, California

Preface

A few words are in order about the overall approach of this book. It is not intended to be just another "price guide," because prices are usually relative to other matters equally important. Points may be appreciated more or less, value-wise, in different parts of the country. Unlike coins and more like diamonds, each point is unique in itself. Indeed, even aware and experienced collectors may place disparate values on any one point. Still, some basic considerations remain, and it is not likely that a poor specimen would be valued as one far better, whatever the type, wherever the location. Fair market values were sought, and in most cases are in fact represented.

The sections regarding top collector items from various geographical regions (eight in all) presented difficulties and from the collecting angle should be mentioned. Some areas within the regions had less-than-favorable material with which Amerinds could work. Such points are generally not as heavily collected as those from some other areas like the Midwest, and are studied more for their utilitarian than artwork value.

Other regions (High Plains) had a relatively sparse prehistoric settlement, or, elsewhere, there were large gaps in life-way chronology, or material other than durable crypto-crystalline for chipping points and blades. Thus the top collector item sections must be viewed with the understanding that they are not nearly equal when compared among themselves.

Like galaxies and vast pinwheels of stars in the universe, North America has unimaginably huge resources of early points and arrowheads, but all land areas were not the same, nor should they be so-considered. All this to a certain extent is reflected in the regional point types, in their variety and quality and even scarcity.

Throughout this book, a wide spectrum of points is presented. There are examples, many of them, under $5.00-10.00, as well as pieces worth hundreds. But an overall balance has been attempted, for these are the points the collector is likely to encounter, and in values the active collector can probably afford. For the most part, this is the broad central quality range, with numerous examples both above and below.

Author's Note

Values listed are not to be considered offers to sell, for generally the points and blades shown are not for sale. The dollar figures, expressly given for this book, are an indication of fair market value, what a point might change hands for between two knowledgeable collectors.

The value is also a strong, if individualistic, appraisal of the piece as a highly collectible object, an analysis of typical worth. Any figures given should be examined with these considerations in mind.

In order to make this book as accurate, detailed, and informative as possible, no known fraudulent or reproduction points are shown, except in the two chapters devoted to the subject. Also, any points known to have been restored will have this fact mentioned.

As a contribution toward preserving this nation's prehistoric heritage – the sites and artifacts – no items known to have been illegally excavated are included. Neither are there any known examples that would counter restrictions of the 1906 Antiquities Act nor ARP/79, the federal Archaeological Resources Protection Act of 1979, or any relevant state statutes. Most examples are legitimate surface finds from across the country.

When the book was being put together, many people wanted to know "what kind" it would be. Basically, there have been three types of publications popularly available. There are booklets for point-type identification, price guides of various kinds, and the quarterly amateur archeological journals. Some helpful studies have been privately published, but they are scarce.

This book, which combines elements of the three mentioned kinds of books, also includes a fourth dimension, arrowheads as art.

Acknowledgments

The writer wishes to thank a number of people whose kind help made this book possible. The named individuals sent photos (many professionally taken) and/or key background information. It is difficult to research a thorough book which deals with all geographic regions of the country without solid input from people living in those regions. This is especially true when such information is not widely available, and in the nature of specialized facts.

It is with pleasure and sincere thanks that the contributors listed here are acknowledged. Their efforts will be noted throughout the book, and the scope of their aid can readily be seen. It is their work, not mine alone, that makes this a book of national coverage, and hopefully, of importance.

My sincere appreciation to:

Les Ferguson	South Dakota
Richard Warren	Missouri
Billy Hillen	Ohio
Robert Hammond	Alaska
Eugene Heflin	Oregon
Gary Fogelman	Pennsylvania
Art Wesolowski	Arizona
Howard Popkie	Canada
Dale Richter	Illinois
Rodney Peck	North Carolina
Dwain Rogers	Texas
Bob & Gerry Rosberg	Illinois
Joseph D. Love	Tennessee
J.N. Thibault	California
Paul L. Hodges	Louisiana
Sam & Nancy Johnson	Arkansas
Jan Sorgenfrei	Ohio
Cliff Morris	California
Bob Lindaw	New Jersey
Charles D. Meyer	Florida
E. Keith Franc	California
Arnold R. Logan	Texas
Gerald R. Riepl	Kansas
Christopher Crew	Iowa
Robert Hershberger	Indiana
Gary R. Aeh	Ohio
John Kolbe	Minnesota
Marguerite Kernaghan	Colorado
Wayne Parker	Texas
Ben Thompson	Missouri
Private Collectors	Various states

Special acknowledgment is also due John Barry for the Foreword, and to my wife, Sue McClurg Hothem, for much assistance in many areas.

Introduction

Just about everybody knows something or other about Indian arrowheads. They know the points and related chipped object – no longer "Indian relic" but "Amerind artifact" – can be found almost anywhere and are widely collected by people of all ages. They realize these fascinating pieces from long ago times can be purchased at yard sales, flea markets, antique shops or shows, and at auctions of many kinds. Arrowheads and projectile points are not only a part of American folklore, but items very much in demand today.

These chipped artifacts probably exist in the uncounted billions, and can be collected in every region of the country. They in fact make up at least 95 percent of all the authentic Amerind pieces that can be collected.

This is a field that is attracting large numbers of younger collectors because of the great availability and variety of chipped artifacts, and often, the relatively low values for some points.

The writer, a point collector for over 25 years, has long been intrigued with arrowheads, lancepoints and blades. Only a relatively few people thoroughly understand this collecting field, and too often points tend to be underpriced or overvalued, or increasingly, fake.

What really are the bold and subtle considerations that make, say, three specimens each 2 inches long respectively worth $5.00, $45.00, and $125.00? This book will explore four things: What is available and where, what is being paid, what's good – and why.

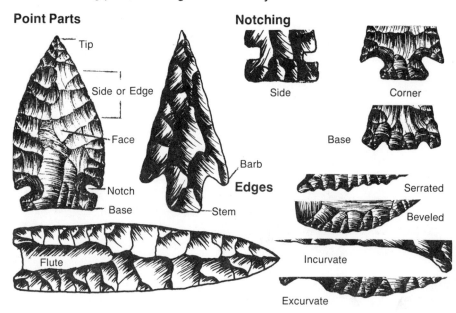

Point Parts

Tip

Side or Edge

Face

Notch

Base

Flute

Barb

Stem

Notching

Side

Corner

Base

Edges

Serrated

Beveled

Incurvate

Excurvate

Dating

The dating method used throughout the book is the standard BC-AD determinations. For a general explanation, we can consider this to be the year 2000 or AD 2000. Time is counted "down" in the BC years (1000, 999, 998, etc.) and "up" in the AD years (1000, 1001, 1002, etc.). There was a statistical meeting point of BC-0-AD that occurred about 2,000 years ago, at least in theory.

To find the true age of any BC figure, add 2000 (0 to AD 2000) to it. For the age of any AD figure, subtract that number from 2000 (the present). The result gives "how long ago" in time, usually blocks of years; in prehistoric time, a closeness of a century is considered quite accurate.

For example, 1500 BC was 3,500 years ago, while AD 1500 was 500 years ago. The time "distance" between these particular BC/AD figures is thus 3,000 years. The authors of some "Suggested Reading" in the following chapters use the designation "BP" to mean Before Present, giving years of age without the possible confusion inherent in the BC/AD system. BP makes 5000 BC into 7000 BP, while AD 200 becomes 1800 BP; AD 2000 becomes, charmingly, 0 BP.

Coverage of each geographic region includes a short introduction to the area, and a listing of states (in the case of Canada, provinces). This will serve as a brief grounding in that area's prehistoric lifeway, and provide some point information. Introductions conclude with a listing of recommended books. These will be helpful to those who wish to learn more about the region in general, and projectile points in particular.

The most important feature of Chapters II through IX, in the author's opinion, are the numerous fine photographs of regional points. These will give not only a good idea of the value of points to collectors, but will provide information in the following areas:

A) Regional point materials
B) Regional point styles and sizes
C) A survey of types (named points)
D) U.S. point similarities and differences
E) Points are prehistoric North American art

In these chapters, key information will be in the photographs, almost all of which are published in these pages for the first time. In addition, detailed captions provide as much background information as is available.

I. THE COLLECTING FIELD

"Arrowheads" have long been a part of our cultural heritage. The word is in common use, in place names (Lake Arrowhead), in products from canoes to food to tools, and advertising (Shawnee Pottery's original company mark). Even the Federal government has recognized the association of arrowheads and primitive surroundings and early peoples. Visitors to U.S. national parks are greeted by signs in the shape of an Indian projectile point, and park personnel wear an arrowhead patch.

The selection of the arrowhead shape was significant. According to Edwin C. Bearss, Chief Historian of the National Parks Service, U.S. Department of the Interior, it was done for several reasons: "Because the National Park Service preserves natural and historic resources, it is appropriate to have an emblem representing both. The arrowhead shape reflects the human history commemorated in our parks; the trees and mountains with the arrowhead symbolize the great natural features in our custody. The shield-like form of the arrowhead effectively contains the agency lettering and associated design. The insignia was adopted in 1952."

The National Park Service did well to choose the arrowhead emblem, for no one has trouble understanding the meaning. Here, the symbols promise, is land with both integrity and spectacular scenery, land true to the way it has always been. It recalls an era when man took only what was needed, and left the remainder to become more. The simple elegance of a prehistoric point echoes the past and reflects the present.

More and more – whether in literature, the media, in collecting Indian artifacts – Native American works are appreciated. This is a fairly recent acknowledgment of, and accomplishment for, the point collector. That person is now seen in a new and positive light, but it was not always that way.

Not too long ago, before about 1960, those who had a serious interest in "old Indian flints" also had a problem. Hardly anyone else was interested. The genuine collector, with a consuming passion to acquire and know about cultural debris from the prehistoric era, was rather alone.

Most people saw such fascination as being a bit strange, an interest and activity pursued by march-to-your-own-drummer individualists. The occasional wealthy person who engaged in a similar pursuit was either ignored or humored. Pre-1960, this imaginary comment could sum up the attitude: "Oh, he's a nice guy, but he collects arrowheads." Non-collectors knew little or nothing about the chipped objects, so there was an added aura of mystery.

Further, the respect engendered by money wasn't present. A common field grade arrowhead was worth a dime to a quarter, if a buyer could be found. Blades 6-inches long, of finest workstyle and material, could be had for a few dollars.

One could even walk out into a field (so non-collectors believed) and pick up the things by the pocketful for nothing. What was free couldn't be worth much, and collecting such things had almost no status.

Sometime shortly after the mid-1960's, this changed. A large number of people gradually became interested in prehistoric points, which farmers had been picking up as curiosities since the late 1700's. The shift in interest and attitude was not overnight, but it was broad and permanent.

This collector-interest developed into competition, creating market demand, and values shot ever upward. Arrowheads and projectile points as good collectibles produced prices that would have made old-time collectors snort in disbelief.

Education helped, and collectors finally began to know what they saw. What once brought 50 cents "because the base isn't all there" now brings a hundred dollars because the type is a rare Paleo form. The main portion of a "broken flint" once worth nothing, now is something of both interest and value, well worth being professionally restored. In the common perception, something known to have been chipped by prehistoric peoples is no longer garbage, but an art object.

Today, riding on this grand turn of events, people collect chipped objects they really should not, points that even if old and authentic, are hardly worth the effort, let alone the money. Some do acquire good pieces, but at a cost far beyond present or potential worth, no matter how it is figured. The person who collects prehistoric points is now accorded a certain prestige, and is admired as someone with awareness in an art area that few others comprehend.

The shift in perception of the collector, once-was to what-is, is healthy, but still needs a balance. The points are considered to be prehistoric, Native American art works, and so they are. But, not all art is necessarily good. Some pieces are superb, others very good, some mediocre, and others (for a variety of reasons) may not be very good at all, and may in fact be bad art.

Today's point collector tends to be somewhat of a specialist, and the collecting field is huge. The basic (perhaps beginning) collector tends to acquire points personally found, surface-hunting favorite sites. The collection grows via trades with other local collectors, or by purchases from a number of sources.

Locally acquired material can be somewhat limited in variety, but the benefit is that points are authentic. In time, and with experience, the collector knows in advance what to expect in the way of area acquisitions, knows what was and was not made in early times. In the overall assemblage, the artifacts of ancient communities are well-represented. This is the basic collection, and there are probably in excess of half a million of them across the country.

Another (not always the next) stage is increasing attraction to one or several collecting areas, and a list would be almost endless. Point collectors are as varied as the ancient cultural items they preserve. Some like highly colorful or translucent material, and point or blade configuration is secondary.

Others like size, and collect mainly long points, or one of a few type ("name") points from certain regions, or artifacts made of one material. Still others like small gem-points, for the perfect work done in miniature. No matter what the collecting emphasis, each point class has both attraction and appeal.

Some advanced collectors, many steps up the awareness and experience ladder, have multifaceted assemblages of chipped artifacts that can be considered the best of the very best. For them, one resists the term "collector's collector," but the description is valid if unavoidable. There are probably only a few hundred such true authorities in chipped art. The average collector may know them only by name and reputation, and such persons are objects of considerable awe.

These collections have the pieces average collectors only dream about: a fluted-base ceremonial-grade Clovis-variant 6" long ($1,300.00); late-Paleo drill in black glossy flint, 4½" long ($900.00); the Oregon gem-point, 1¼" long ($225.00); the St. Charles "dovetail" in translucent Flintridge ($850.00); the leaf-shaped *cache* blade, 10" long ($1,100.00). Are "arrowheads" really worth (Chapter XXII) this kind of money? They are to the people that pay it.

Unlike many other types of Amerind collectibles – rugs, pottery and pipe-tomahawks, to mention three – point collecting does not need to be an expensive hobby, avocation or diversion. For most, the supreme enjoyment does not lie in how much the collection is, or will be, worth. Collecting is not a private club, and anyone can take part. The only required degrees are those of attraction and interest. For those of us who collect projectile points and related chipped art, it is the most satisfying possible.

II. THE NORTHEAST

(Connecticut, Delaware, Maine, Maryland, Massachusetts, New Hampshire, New Jersey, New York, Pennsylvania, Rhode Island, Vermont, Virginia, West Virginia)

Amerind occupation in the Northeast began early, and dates of 14,000 BC have been assigned to the Meadowcroft rockshelter near Pittsburgh, Pennsylvania. These earliest Paleo hunters occasionally brought down giant animals now extinct, but a reliance on elk and caribou is indicated for the region. Their chipped artifacts were fluted base points and numerous knives and scrapers.

The Archaic period, a hunting and food-gathering time, lasted from 8000-1500 BC, similar to the eastern Midwest. These peoples are important to the collector, for – as compared with the scarcity of Paleo points – the Archaic period provided a great range of points and point types.

These include the typical bifurcates, corner and side-notched lanceheads, plus a number of knife types. A greater quantity of points indicates a higher dependence on hunting. The wider the style variations (types), usually the larger the number of cultural groups that hunted.

Transitional cultures followed the Archaic, with a growing and changing lifeway increasingly dependent on crop-raising and pottery. These were the Woodland times. This lasted from centuries before BC-0-AD until ca. AD 1000, and points tended to be larger and less varied than the multitude of Archaic forms.

The New England area of the Northeast did not possess a wealth of high-quality point materials, and some lower-grade materials were worked. By AD 1000, the Woodland era with the *Atl-atl,* pottery and agriculture had been largely replaced by bow-and-arrow people. Their points were much smaller and, as elsewhere, were often simple unnotched triangular forms, or notched or stemmed.

Major contact with Europeans began in the AD 1500's, and the old lifeways became but memories. As in other U.S. regions, it is not precisely known when chipped objects lost their appeal and their use with Indians. But they were replaced as White-made iron, steel and firearms became generally available.

Suggested reading:

Fowler, William S. *Classification of Stone Implements of the Northeast.* Massachusetts Archaeological Society, Inc., Attleboro, Maine, 1963.

Handbook of North American Indians: NORTHEAST. Smithsonian Institution, Volume 15, Washington, DC, 1978.

Brewerton corner-notched, Archaic, Kalberg flint. All are from New Jersey, with average length of 2¼." Values: $4.00-$30.00. (Bob Lindaw Collection, New Jersey; Joe Hodulik photo)

Bifurcates, Archaic era, made of Normanskill, Kalberg or Kittatinny flints. From 1½"-2¾" long, all are from New Jersey. Values: $1.00 (bottom right); $25.00 (top left). (Bob Lindaw Collection, New Jersey; Joe Hodulik photo)

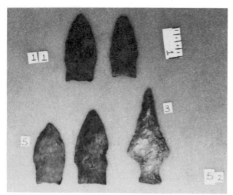

Northeastern points (see inch-scale for size.) The four similar examples, late Paleo, are known to PA collectors as Fox Creek Stemmed or Fox Creek Lanceolates. Usually of argillite, these are of a grey slate-like material. The point or blade (bottom right) is an Ashtabula, a type which ranges from crude to refined and is from the Archaic time frame. Values: $8.00-$30.00. (Gary Fogelman Collection, Pennsylvania)

Snookkill points, of Kalberg flint, transitional type. From New York, these have slight, rounded stems and angular shoulders. Values: $5.00-$10.00 each. (Bob Lindaw Collection, New Jersey; Joe Hodulik photo)

Northeastern Broadpoints of the following types, with average specimen about 2": Perkioman, Susquehanna Broad, and Lobate-stemmed Broads. Materials are mostly rhyolite, center point of brown jasper, others local grey or black composite. These points are typically valued at $5.00-$20.00. (Gary Fogelman Collection, Pennsylvania)

Orient fishtails, New Jersey, 1500-1000 BC; center piece, 2⅛" flint. Point values: $8.00-25.00 each. (Kernaghan Collection, Colorado; Stewart W. Kernaghan, photographer)

Levanna points, AD 900-1350, of flint, jasper and quartzite. Values: $5.00-$15.00 each; a basic triangular arrowhead. (Kernaghan Collection, Colorado; Stewart W. Kernaghan, photographer)

Quartz points, longest 2", from New Jersey, Archaic period. Values: $3.00-$8.00 each. (Kernaghan Collection, Colorado; Marguerite Kernaghan, photographer)

Poplar Island points, Archaic, black flint and (third from left) shale. From New Jersey, these artifacts average 3" long. Values: $9.00-$25.00 each. (Bob Lindaw Collection, New Jersey; Joe Hodulik photo)

Gadsden, 2⁷⁄₁₆", Woodland, low-grade cream-colored chert. Point is almost totally percussion-flaked, giving a certain rough look. It is from Polk County, Florida. Value: $18.00. (Private Collection, Florida)

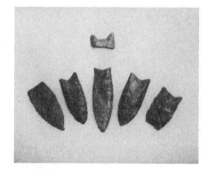

Northeastern Paleos, center point is over 3" long. Left to right, after top: Clovis basal fragment, Lanceolate, $40.00-$50.00. Clovis, fluted, damage, $150.00-$185.00. Center: Clovis variant, $300.00-$400.00. Clovis, $225.00-$275.00. Fragment is of little value. (Gary Fogelman Collection, Pennsylvania)

Bolen beveled (subtype 2), early Archaic, 2" long, semi-glossy tan flint. Strongly beveled, fine serrations, from Polk County, Florida. Value: $35.00. (Private Collection, Florida)

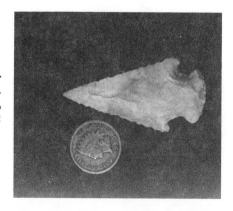

Orient fishtail points and blades, all from New Jersey. The majority are made of argillite, plus shale or jasper. Values: $5.00-$35.00. (Bob Lindaw Collection, New Jersey; Joe Hodulik photo)

Otter Creek blades, flint or argillite, 4" average length. All are from Albany County, New York. Values: (from left to right) $13.00, $30.00, $11.00 and $13.00. (Bob Lindaw Collection, New Jersey; Joe Hodulik photo)

Lackawaxen points or blades, average length 2⅞". From New Jersey, material is a grey slate. Values: $5.00-$25.00. (Bob Lindaw Collection, New Jersey; Joe Hodulik photo)

Otter Creek blade, Normanskill flint, 5". This piece has excellent design, fine base and size, from New York. Value: $125.00-$175.00. (Bob Lindaw Collection, New Jersey; Joe Hodulik photo)

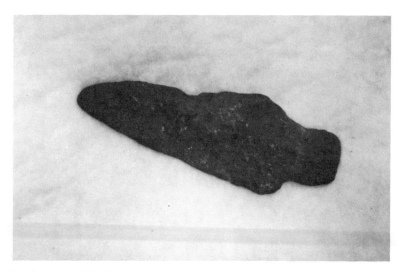

Lackawaxen blade, just over 4", made of Eastern slate. The rounded tip and shoulders are typical; Archaic period. Value: $5.00. (Private collection)

Blades, stemmed, 3", dense slate-like chert. Top left: blade, diminished stem, tip missing. $2.00. Bottom right: blade, better form, equally undistinguished material. $5.00. These examples do not mean the chippers were unskilled, but that the material did not work well. (Private collection)

Normanskill blades made of flint, shale and quartzite, all from New York. Of Archaic origin, the type is quite long for width. Values: $8.00-$15.00 each. (Bob Lindaw Collection, New Jersey; Joe Hodulik photo)

Slate blade, 3" about ¼" thick. From the New England area, basic form is good, but left-base damage detracts. Ground and polished points or blades are generally more valuable than chipped slate. Worth here is $5.00-$6.00. (Private collection)

Northeastern scrapers, flake and snub-nosed, average large example about 2". In many colors, they are from Lycoming and Northumberland Counties, Pennsylvania. Scrapers of all types are collectible, but like so many other aspects of the field, degree of interest varies with the individual. Values begin at several dollars. (Gary Fogelman Collection, Pennsylvania)

III. THE SOUTHEAST
(Alabama, Arkansas, Florida, Georgia, Louisiana, Mississippi, North Carolina, South Carolina, Tennessee)

Again, it was the free-roaming Paleo hunters who left their distinctive points as signposts of the first known human occupation on this non-glaciated terrain. Ancient skeletons in Florida have been found in isolated graves, indicating an age perhaps earlier than standard time-period given of 9000-8000 BC. Most point forms are of two types, the early concave-base Clovis-like, and the slender, dagger-shaped lanceolate.

By 6000 BC, the Archaic lifeway was in full development, with the usual widespread food base that supplemented the hunting of game animals, especially deer. While each region has its common points, some of the coastal regions also contain points obviously made in the U.S. interior. The Southeast is no exception, and it is almost as if the early Archaic people spread their points (by travel or trade) as far as they could, to the edge of the great salt sea.

Beginning around 1000 BC, the Woodland period accented village life and the building of mounds. This conservative lifeway seems to have been directed at elaborate burial ceramics and ceremonies, culminating in the Southern Death Cult with fine grave goods. Points and blades by then went in two directions. There were the utilitarian points, medium-large, stemmed or notched, and fantastic ceremonial/burial objects.

The Temple Mound period began about AD 1200 and brought a new surge of social/religious activity with huge ceremonial centers with imposing mounds. Some resembled the Mesoamerican pyramids, and perhaps the idea came from Mexico. Other than projectile points, this people also chipped adzes, celts and chisels from flint, polishing the edges to a high shine.

Some ultra-fine objects were chipped, the likes of which were not made elsewhere. These include giant sword-like blades up to several feet long, and batons or maces. There were also monolithic axes, elaborate head and handle chipped from one piece of flint. Most examples are represented in the famous Duck River cache of large chipped artifacts.

Eventually the bow-wielding Mississippian peoples began to dominate the land. Living in small villages with palisade walls, they were a hunting and agricultural people. Whites arrived early in the 1500's, and the disintegration of Native groups began.

Suggested reading:

Bierer, Bert W. *Indian Artifacts in the Southeast – A Sketchbook.* Privately published, Columbia, South Carolina, 1977.

Lewis, Thomas M.N., and Madeline Kneberg. *Tribes That Slumber – Indians of the Tennessee Region.* The University of Tennessee Press, Knoxville, Tennessee, 1973.

Peck, Rodney M. *Indian Projectile Types From Virginia and The Carolinas.* (From 2121 Quail Drive, Harrisburg, North Carolina 28075), 1982.

Cumberland points, early fluted-face artifacts, ca. 8000 BC. Like the Folsom, they are fluted from base to tip. Unlike it, they are much longer and less wide, earred rather than barbed, and the two are generally found in different regions. These scarce points have style, workmanship and rarity in their favor. This point grouping would have an average per-piece value of at least $650.00 since they would be (to most collectors) comparable in appeal. (Joseph D. Love Collection, Tennessee)

Plevna blades, largest specimen nearly 5". Photo shows the wide size range for this knife type. These examples, ca. 4000 BC, have typical beveled knife-edges and are sturdily constructed. Value range is from $15.00 (far right) to $250.00 (far left). Midwestern collectors will note a resemblance to certain "dovetails." (Joseph D. Love Collection, Tennessee)

Eccentric flints, like this 2" long example, have no known purpose and very few were made in prehistoric times. Values for such odd-shaped items vary, but is not usually high. (Joseph D. Love Collection, Tennessee)

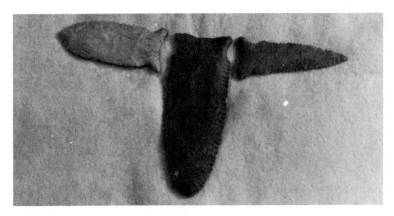

Greenbrier blades, ca. 4500 BC. These are large and extremely well-finished examples, a centerpiece to any collection. Left: good ears, overall aesthetics, $150.00. Center: a superb 4" blade, very regular edge-chipping, fine size for type, balanced. This blade, in writer's opinion, could not really have been better made, $700.00. Right: slender form indicates much resharpening but lines are still excellent and well serrated, $125.00. As in all Amerind chipped art, the reason why the large piece is worth three times more than the smaller ones is a matter of perception and aesthetics. (Joseph D. Love Collection, Tennessee)

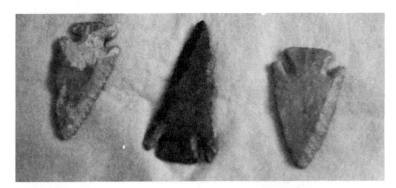

Lost Lake blades, about 3", an early Archaic knife similar to several other beveled-edged blades. Of good material, well-designed, with superior work-styles, such pieces deserve collector attention. Values: (left to right) $75.00, $400.00 and $150.00. (Joseph D. Love Collection, Tennessee)

Kirk corner-notch, 5⅝", North Carolina, Archaic. Made of local dark grey silicified shale. Fine secondary flaking implies that specimen might have been used as knife. $165.00. (Rodney Peck; Harrisburg, North Carolina)

Clovis, 4¾" x 1½", from Rhea County, Tennessee. Material is a speckled grey, orange and tan flint. Clipping and edge treatment are extremely fine and condition is perfect. Points or blades of this age and quality are rarely encountered. When edge has been smoothed to this extent and tip has been left a bit rounded, this may denote a ceremonial piece. $700.00-$900.00. (Robert Hammond Collection, Alaska)

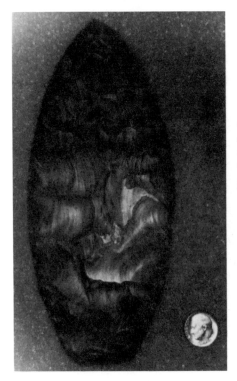

Caddoan blade, square-back, 7¼", ca. AD 1250-1400, from Arkansas. Made of Woodward chert, it has fine length, balanced excurvate sides, and is very finely worked on both faces and all edges. This is a highly artistic piece, ceremonial grade, and an important flint from the period. "Very valuable." (Sam and Nancy Johnson Collection, Arkansas)

Scottsbluff-I, from Arkansas, about 3½". An early type, it has a good outline in lanceolate form. Value: $150.00-$225.00. (Paul L. Hodges Collection, Louisiana)

23

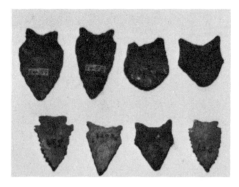

San Patrice points, Louisiana. Photo illustrates five of the point varieties. Generally late Archaic, most have prominent basal ears. Longest specimen is about 2" and values average $8.00-$20.00. (Paul L. Hodges Collection, Louisiana)

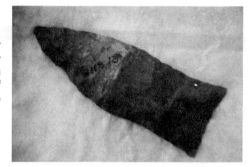

Blade or point, probably reworked Copena, ca. AD 500, average 3". Of bluish flint, there is a material change for about ⅖ of length, of a lighter, less attractive flint, $15.00. (Private collection)

This Clovis is a very large size (5½" x 1¾") for this early point type. From Humphreys County, Tennessee, it is made of dark Dover flint and surface is weathered. Outline for this major piece is excellent, as is the chipping done by this early hunting people. The basal flute is good, and the piece is a fine combination of features. $800.00-$1,000.00. (Robert Hammond Collection, Alaska)

Point varieties. Top right: unknown point, 2¼", tip area damaged (probably Paleo time frame) $7.50. Bottom left: Beaver Lake-like point, tip damage, drab material, age patina, $10.00. (Private collection)

Scottsbluff-type, ⅞" x 4¾", Hale County, Alabama, of opalized rhyolite. It has good size and lines, perfect condition, $350.00. (Kernaghan Collection, Colorado; Marguerite Kernaghan, photo-grapher)

Beaver-tails from Tennessee (largest 1⅜" x 3¼"), all of high-grade chert. These are robust points with strong stems, reflecting conservative Adena times. Serrated point at right may be a Dickson variant. These dart-points are each in the $40.00-$55.00 range. (Kernaghan Collection, Colorado; Marguerite Kernaghan, photographer)

Southeastern points, largest 1⅛" x 3¼" (lower right). Types are Copena (top left), Beaver Lake (lower left), lanceolate (center and center left), and stemmed lanceolate (lower right). Values are in the $15.00-$60.00 range; all points from Tennessee. (Kernaghan Collection, Colo-rado; Marguerite Kernaghan, photographer)

Susquehanna broad points, Pennsylvania, 1200-700 BC, largest piece 1" x 1½". Good flint grades, perfect condition for these attractive points. Values: $20.00-$40.00 each. (Kernaghan Collection, Colo-rado; Marguerite Kernaghan, photographer)

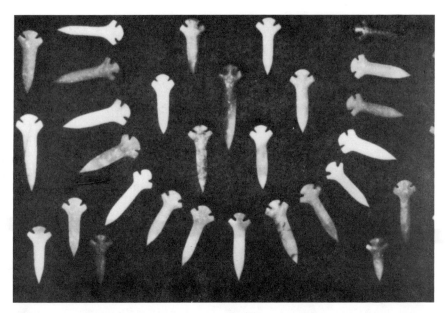

Agee points, classic style, average length 2". This fine assemblage, from Miller County, Arkansas, is of highly colorful Arkansas novaculite. Note the unusual but very artistic lines of this point type, each piece extremely well-chipped. Values: $150.00-$500.00. (Sam and Nancy Johnson Collection, Arkansas)

Copena blades, averaging 3", are made with excurvate-incurvate edges (AD 500.) These are well-made pieces, and size and quality material make them attractive. Values for such examples would be about $50.00 (far right) to $275.00 (far left). (Joseph D. Love Collection, Tennessee)

St. Albans points, early Archaic, from Virginia and North Carolina, average size a bit under 2". These are bifurcated-base points, of silicified shale, quartz and quartzite. Value range is from $10.00-$40.00 depending on size, work-style, condition, etc. (Rodney Peck; Harrisburg, North Carolina)

Clovis point, made of very unusual material, crystal quartz. This scarce example is 1¾" long and was found near Boydton, Virginia. Good lines for this hard-to-work and attractive material. $200.00. (Rodney Peck; Harrisburg, North Carolina)

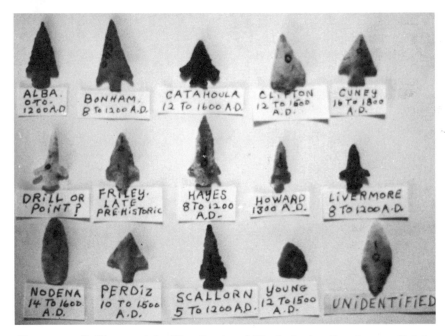

These are all AD-era points, Woodland and Mississippian time frames. Points average 1½". Top row (left to right): Alba, $8.00; Bonham, $15.00; Catahoula, $25.00; Clifton, $5.00; Cuney, AD 1600-1800, $12.00. Second row (left to right): Drill, winged, $35.00; Friley, $8.00; Hayes, sharp tip, $25.00; Howard, narrow arrowhead form, $8.00; Livermore, $10.00. Third row (left to right): Nodena, leaf-shaped, $20.00; Perdiz, wide-shouldered, $11.00; Scallorn, serrated, $15.00, Young, $5.00; Unknown point, $6.00. (Paul L. Hodges Collection, Louisiana)

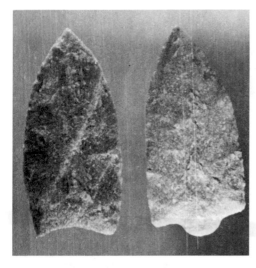

Southeastern Archaic period. Left: unidentified point, 5½", made of grey quartzite with concave base and good balance, $150.00. Right: Morrow Mountain, 5½", made of grey quartzite with good workmanship, $150.00. (Rodney Peck; Harrisburg, North Carolina)

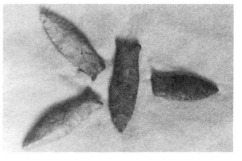

Beaver Lake points, these averaging 3", are a type also known as "non-fluted" Cumberland due to length, narrowness and basal ears. They are ca. 7000 BC. Surprisingly thick for Paleo points, they yet have a graceful, flowing form. These examples would be in the $75.00-$200.00 range. (Joseph D. Love Collection, Tennessee)

Guilford point, black flint, picked up on a North Carolina beach site, somewhat worn by wave action. This piece, 3¼", is middle Archaic, ca. 4500 BC, $15.00. (Private collection)

Lanceolate, late Paleo form, 3" long, pale brown flint from Tennessee. Good form and condition, material a bit grainy, condition better than average, $25.00. (Private collection)

Pee Dee points, Southeast, after ca. AD 1550. Points are just over 1¼" long. These have a pentagonal or five-sided outline. Left: well-chipped, slender, $7.00. Right: wider, more common type, $13.00. (Private collection)

Dismal Swamp points, Viriginia, Archaic, found around the Great Dismal Swamp area. Points are 1½"-2" long, and are made of multicolored chalcedony. Value range for these points is from $5.00-$15.00 depending on size and workmanship. Left: $5.00; right: $10.00; center: $12.00. (Rodney Peck; Harrisburg, North Carolina)

Hardaway point, 1⅛" with characteristic very wide and concave base and large basal-thinning flakes that resemble flutes. Not a common point and in perfect condition, $25.00. (Private collection)

Savannah River, 4⅞", from Mecklenburg County, North Carolina, late Archaic period. Material is brown silicified shale; good size for this piece, $100.00. (Rodney Peck; Harrisburg, North Carolina)

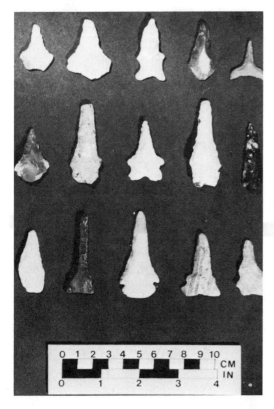

A collection of 15 drills from North Carolina and Virginia, dating from Archaic to Woodland periods. Materials are silicified shale, flint and quartz. Values: $4.00-$50.00. Note: "The value of the artifacts are approximate and vary depending on location, material, size and workmanship. Example: A North Carolina collector will pay more for a local piece than one of equal size and workmanship from another state" – RMP. (Rodney Peck; Harrisburg, North Carolina)

Morrow Mountain, 4⅝", Archaic, from Buckroe Beach, Virginia. Material is weathered white rhyolite. Note highly unusual basal configuration compared with other blades, $75.00. (Rodney Peck; Harrisburg, North Carolina)

Lost Lake, 4", from Virginia. Material is a dark grey silicified shale. This piece has very good workmanship and a superb configuration, very well balanced, $350.00. (Rodney Peck; Harrisburg, North Carolina)

Oleta points from north central Louisiana, ca. 4000-2000 BC. Averaging 1½" long, it is a recently named type. The Oleta has large notching, excurvate sides and both faces have a large "dished out" percussion flake scar, or several. This may be an unsettled transitional form. Value range for this point is $6.00-$12.00. (Paul L. Hodges Collection, Louisiana)

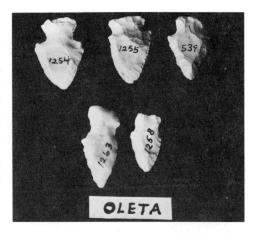

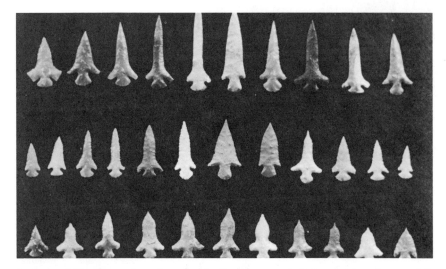

Agee and Homan points from early Caddoan and Colescreek cultures, AD 200-800. Length: smallest example is 1¼" long. The materials are Arkansas no-vaculite and Arkansas golden jasper. These are superb points, with values from $75.00 (smallest) to $350.00 (largest) and higher. (Ex. coll. Sam Johnson, Arkansas)

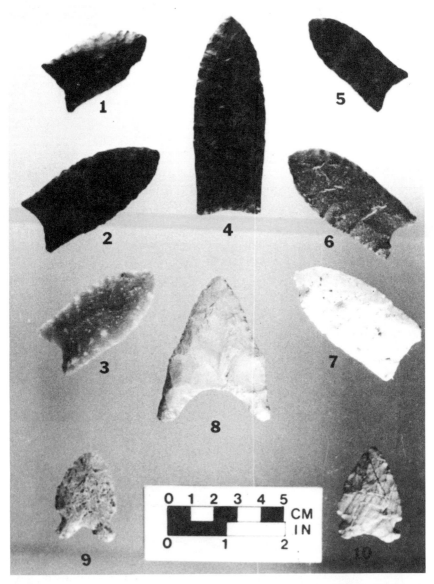

North Carolina chipped art (1-10), see scale for size. 1) Clovis, North Carolina, material dark green silicified shale, $130.00. 2) Clovis, Forsyth Country, green silicified shale, $200.00. 3) Clovis, Surry County, gold translucent agate, $200.00. 4) Clovis, Bladen County, in brown Dover flint, $500.00. 5) Clovis, Granville County, black silicified shale, $150.00. 6) Clovis, Rowan County, grey silicified shale, $200.00. 7) Clovis, Alamance County, translucent white chalcedony, $200.00. 8) Alamance, Vance County, weathered green silicified shale, $225.00. 9) Hardaway, Union County, grey quartzite, $35.00. 10) Hardaway, Granville County, banded purple silicified shale, $35.00. (Rodney Peck; Harrisburg, North Carolina)

IV. THE MIDWEST

The Midwest is the only regional chapter in this book to be divided into two sections or subdivisions, and there are some good reasons for doing so. The Midwest is considered to be an Amerind cultural heartland, and human occupation, in relatively large numbers, lasted for over 10,000 years.

This helps explain the wealth of projectile points and their incredible range of styles and variations. As an example of how much material or information there is to be developed, no one has ever published a complete report on prehistoric Midwestern knives or blades, including the named and unnamed types. Point types exist in such numbers that at least half of all known named points can be found, frequently or occasionally, in the eastern and western Midwest.

The region, now comprising seven adjoining states, was highly favorable for Amerinds of whatever time and place. This fact is indicated by long-term occupation of certain small areas, such as the well-known Koster site in Illinois. At this site people lived for over 8,500 years and that was but one of thousands of sites. Some were larger, some smaller.

With attractive climate, plenty of water and the land forested or in grass, a balanced environment was available, one that could be adapted to in different ways. Living, if not easy, was not too difficult. In addition, there was a wide variety of quality flint and cherts for projectile points and blades.

That is one reason why there are so many thousands of non-area collectors who prefer to specialize in Midwestern artifacts, and why such collections can be found almost anywhere in the country.

A) The Eastern Midwest
(Indiana, Kentucky, Michigan, Ohio)

After the retreat of the awesome glacial ice sheets, humans moved in. Some states, like Indiana and Ohio, were only partly glaciated by the Wisconsin advance of some 13,000 years ago, and Amerinds may have existed near such regions in very early times.

Big game hunters were followed, about 8000 BC, by the herd animal hunters, and their long, graceful points are similar to some types found on the Great Plains. Both the lanceolate and fluted-based peoples also chipped long drills, skinning and butchering knives, and several kinds of hide scrapers.

The herd hunters merged into the Archaic times, 7000-1000 BC, an economy of wild food gathering, fishing and hunting. Each time period produced different point designs, and most can be recognized at a glance, at least as to general period. Eastern Midwest collectors have the greatest point selection from Archaic times, since it apparently had a fairly large Amerind population, and lasted for 6,000 years.

Adena and Hopewell agricultural societies developed next – the Adena with their conservative long, stemmed points; the Hopewell with flat points with large concave notches. Both peoples constructed mounds, sometimes with chipped artifacts as grave goods.

Following Woodland times, 1000 BC-AD 1000, the bow people took over the eastern Midwest, and they were the Ft. Ancient, the Erie, and others. Arrowheads (the bow may have arrived in the area ca. AD 800) were usually some form of the simple triangular point, rarely notched, occasionally stemmed, sometimes serrated. The technology suited the times, with agriculture, some hunting and warfare. However, the fantastic array of Archaic chipped points was never duplicated.

Suggested reading:

Prufer, Olaf H. and Raymond S. Baby. *Paleo-Indians of Ohio,* The Ohio Historical Society, Columbus, Ohio, 1963.

Webb, William S. *Indian Knoll* (Kentucky). The University of Tennessee Press, Knoxville, Tennessee, (reprint) 1974.

Blade, 4⅛", in translucent pink flint. The knife resembles some Table Rock types, though basal damage precludes more positive identification. This is a large and well-made piece, Midwestern, $175.00. (Hershberger Collection, Indiana; Jeff Hershberger, photographer)

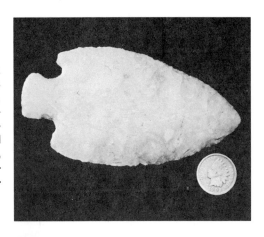

Triangular points, typical for much of the Midwest's late prehistoric period. Central point is 1½" long. Values (left to right): $5.00, $5.00 and $8.00, based on workstyle. (Lar Hothem photo)

Late prehistoric arrowheads, center specimen ⅞" long. A number of Midwestern groups made similar points, many corner-notched in some fashion. Point value (left to right) $6.00, $7.00 and $8.00, based on workmanship. (Lar Hothem Collection)

Blades or knives, Midwestern, lower center piece 3¼". Photo illustrates the range of materials and styles that good points should evidence. These are mainly Archaic-era types, and pieces are in the $20.00-$150.00 range. (Hershberger Collection, Indiana; Jeff Hershberger, photographer)

Midwestern blade types, various flints and cherts. Top row: (left to right) Copena, 4", AD 300, Kentucky, $45.00; Snyder, 2½", BC-0-AD, Missouri, $70.00. Middle Row: (left to right) Adena, 5", late BC/early AD years, Illinois, $85.00; Plevna, 3", 6000 BC, Kentucky, $95.00. Bottom row: (left to right) Sedalia, 4", est. 5000 BC, Missouri, $65.00; Thebes, 2¼", 7000 BC, Illinois, $70.00. (Cliff Morris Collec-tion, California; photo by Ray Pace, Associates)

Unknown point, probably Woodland, deeply concave base, 2¼" long. A very well-chipped piece, good lines and balance, perfect condition, $35.00. (Lar Hothem Collection)

Midwestern fine flint, Paleo and Archaic pieces, with large stemmed lanceolate at center, a type often found in broken or badly damaged condition. The dark-colored flints widely used in pre-Woodland times are well-illustrated here. (Old Barn Auction, Find Lay,Ohio)

Midwestern flint, late-Paleo to Adena times, all perfect and in finest material grades. Leaf-blade at center has strong color contrast, usually as here a plus factor. Points and blades of this quality often are valued at $200.00-$700.00 each. (Old Barn Auction FindLay, Ohio)

Eastern Midwest flint, Paleo through Adena times, in a variety of materials and period cultural styles. The average point or blade here would be valued at close to $550.00 due to size, condition and fine materials. Bottom row identification (left to right): Late Adena, fluted-base Paleo, Archaic bevel-edge, and two Woodland leaf-shaped blades. (Old Barn Auction, FindLay, Ohio)

Midwestern flint, Paleo to Woodland period, in a great range of styles and materials. Value range per piece is extreme, $30.00-$900.00. Condition on all points and blades is perfect. (Old Barn Auction, FindLay Ohio)

Midwestern flint, Archaic and Adena periods, all in fine condition, in top-grade materials. The superb Dovetail blade at center would be valued by many collectors at $1,200.00 and above. (Old Barn Auction FindLay, Ohio)

Exceptional Midwestern flint, with the three large center blades especially impres-sive. Large blades can be valued at $300.00-$750.00 smaller blades from $50.00-$350.00. (Old Barn Auction FindLay Ohio,)

Midwestern blades – large, perfect and fine. Left: Archaic side-notch, Woodland leaf-shaped. Right: Archaic Dovetail. Blades com-parable to left and right examples can be valued at from $500.00-$1,200.00. (Old Barn Auctio FindLay, Ohio)

St. Charles blades, center specimen over 4". Left to right: Dovetail, well-serrated edging, $150.00. Dovetail, balanced notching, uniform edges, well-grounded and shaped base. Values for such pieces start at several hundred dollars. Dovetail with one edge nick has an excellent "dove" base and quality flint, $200.00. (Private collection)

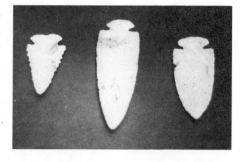

Bifurcates – an array of artifacts that illustrate the size/style range of this early form. Top row (left to right): Point, 1" long, $12.00; Point, well-serrated, $35.00; Point, highly unusual form, adding to rarity, $30.00. Blade with original use marks, $45.00 due to size, canted blade and basal size/design. (Private collection)

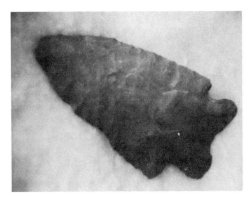

Blade, corner-notched Archaic, 3⅜" long, made of brown flint with an incurvate base. This is a typical specimen, good excurvate edge to top side; irregular edge outline on other, shoulder differences, tip damage, excellent chipping overall, $45.00. (Lar Hothem Collection)

Point, late Paleo rechipped lanceolate with early find data and dated March 16, 1921. This piece is old and good, made of a white, chalky chert, $12.00. Note: Fake historic inscriptions are beginning to appear on some points, both authentic and reproduction. (Lar Hothem Collection)

Arrowheads, late prehistoric, made from flakes, ⅞" long, a type known as Klunk points. These are fairly early arrowheads, AD 700-800, $8.00 each. (Private Collection)

Ceremonial blade, Illinois, 10¼" long. Red Ochre-related, made of a quality regional chert. Blades of this size command collector attention, especially in such fine condition. Note smoothness of edges, not likely to be found in an utilitarian knife. For such high-quality pieces, values can easily exceed $1,250.00. (Bob and Gerry Rosberg Collection, Illinois)

Blade, 4¹⁄₁₆" long, Flintridge milky chalcedony, probably Archaic. Despite appearance, it is undamaged. Beveled hafting to lower right on bottom edge, prehistoric use marks to left on lower edge. Top edge is very well-formed. Though this is an unbalanced piece, it is the way it was made. Material and length are the main value determinants, $55.00. (Lar Hothem Collection)

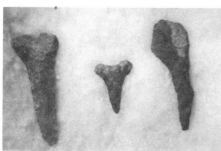

Drill group, eastern Midwest. Left to right: Drill, glossy tan flint, 1¾" long, good lines, but tip and base damage, $7.00; Drill, late Woodland type, perfect, miniature specimen in glossy grey flint, $10.00; Drill or perforator, mixed material, poor chipping, inartistic configuration, an example of what not to collect, $1.50. (Private collection)

Arrowheads – these long, slender forms are also known as Schild points, each 1" long. They are common on late Woodland Indian sites and were bow-propelled. Left: $7.00; center, $5.00; right: $10.00. (Private collection)

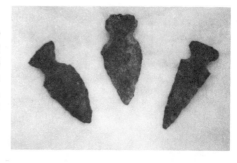

Blades or points. Left to right: Blade, bifurcated base, 1⅞" long, black quality flint, Archaic, unbalanced lobes, shoulder differences, $30.00; Blade, grey glossy flint, Archaic, well made but one base corner projects more than other, $20.50; Blade or point, Woodland, mottled blue-grey flint, short flat-based stem, good lines, $18.00. (Private collection)

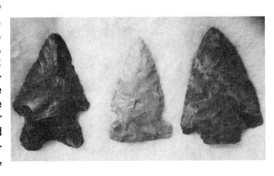

Top: Archaic blade, edges worn, side notched, 3⅜" long. Flint is a glossy black, damage to one basal extension, yet with fair balance to blade body, $50.00. Bottom: Late-Paleo lanceolate, grey flint, 3⅜" long. Artifacts from this early period are often broken due to point length and thinness, so rarity is a value factor here. Smoother side edges would add to aesthetics, $85.00. (Private collection)

Hopewell points, longest 3", Woodland-era. Left: mottled brown and green Flintridge, $125.00. Left center: gem-point in mixed white Flintridge, translucent, $175.00. Center right: very thin, white Flintridge chalcedony, $125.00. Right: pink to white flint, cross-section heavier than others, $115.00. (Gary Aeh Collection, Ohio)

Archaic pieces, ca. 7000-1500 BC in Midwest. Left to right: Bifurcate blade, black flint, 2" long; tip, shoulder and base irregularities, $9.00. Point, pale chert, one shoulder damaged, good ex-coll. mark-ings for state, possibly a point between Paleo and early Archaic times, $8.00. Bifurcate blade, mottled blue flint, balanced base a plus, un- balanced shoulders for a minus, largely undamaged, little basal grinding, $22.50. (Private collection)

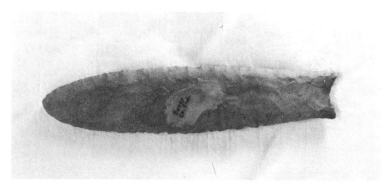

Hazel, a Paleo Cumberland variant, but with short flutes, 5½" x 1¼". Material is a tan flint, and the point or blade comes from Posey County, Indiana. This is a nicely balanced early piece, with good length and overall workstyle. This point type is not common, $750.00-$1200.00. (Robert Hammond Collection, Alaska)

Points, longest 1½", from Illinois. These appear to be stemmed and notched Woodland-era types. All of chert, colors white and pink, white, and tan. Values are in the $5.00-$7.00 range. (Dale Richter Collection, Illinois)

Side-notch blade, Archaic, well-serrated from shoulders to tip, in high-grade flint. 4⅞" long, fine design and workmanship, delicacy and perfection makes this a valuable piece. The collector lists this in excess of $100.00 and actual value could be five times the amount. (Private collection)

Paleo points, center examples 3" long. Left to right: Point, late-Paleo, very similar to Dalton form, $40.00; Stringtown lanceolate, with stem-corner protrusion, dark flint, $95.00; Lanceolate, reworked until edges touch ground-edge hafting area, $20.00. (Billy Hillen Collection, Ohio)

Triangular blades, center example about 3" long. Left to right: Triangular, exceptional thinness, fine flint, $50.00; Triangular, good length for width, attractive material with artistic color contrasts, $85.00; Triangular, reworked or retouched edges to give fine lines, very balanced blade, $80.00. (Private collection)

Corner-notched blade, 4" long, from Ohio. Serrated edges, slight damage to one edge, Coshocton County flint. Well-designed base is heavily ground, with slight base-bottom center notching. This Archaic piece has excellent corner notching, plus fine size, $275.00. (Gary Aeh Collection, Ohio)

Lanceolate, late Paleo, a bit edge worn but with classic lines and size 3¼". This is an "unfluted-fluted" type, quite thin, excellent chipping and material. Unfortunately, parts of the incurvate base seem to have been retouched in later times, but there is debate about whether the reworking is modern. Value: $85.00. (Private collection)

Blade, translucent honey-colored Flintridge, with exquisite attention to base, 2" long. An Archaic serrated edge bevel, the tip appears broken at an angle, but the piece was purposely chipped this way, and it is complete. Value is about $65.00 due to base, serrations and gem-flint material. (Private collection)

43

Drills and reamers, longest piece 1½". From Vermilion County, Illinois, materials are white and brown chert. Values: Left column (top to bottom) $4.00, $4.00, $3.00. Right column (top to bottom) $8.00, $15.00, $8.00. (Dale Richer Collection, Illinois)

Pine Tree point from Kentucky, just over 3" long. This specimen has fine basal and shouldering symmetry, good overall balance. One side was used more than the other, wearing down serrations. Pine Tree points are probably middle Archaic, ca. 3500 BC, and are found on the eastern fringes of the Midwest. This example is chipped from blue-grey flint. Value: $175.00-225.00. (Ben Thompson Collection; St. Louis, Missouri)

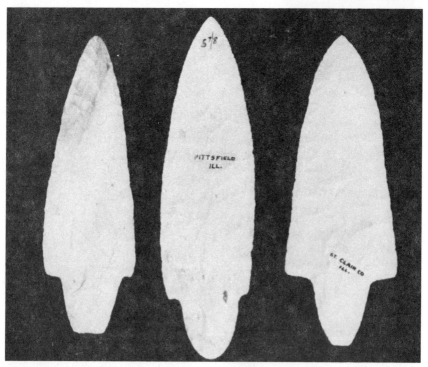

Dickson points or blades, all from Illinois. Center specimen is 5⅞" long. Materials: (left to right) pink chert, white chert and cream-colored chert. Each has slightly differing shouldering and basal configurations. Note excellent outlines of these pieces, good size and fine condition, plus top workstyle – all things collectors seek. Value range: $500.00-$650.00 each. (Ben Thompson Collection; St. Louis, Missouri)

Blades and points, Kentucky. Knives in photo are 5" long. Age period Archaic (notched types) to Ft. Ancient (triangular). Group value (helpful figure when purchasing a small collection) is $100.00-$150.00. (Dale Richter Collection, Illinois)

Pentagonals, longest example about 2". Named this because of the five sides (base, upper edges, lower edges). They are not common. Despite average length of less than 2", these are probably small knives due to the robust and thick bases and resharpening mainly on the upper edge portions. Late Archaic, these well-made examples are in the $10.00-$25.00 range. (Billy Hillen Collection)

Exceptional blades, all eastern Midwest Archaic period, ca. 7000-2000 BC. Side notch, very regular edging, mottled quality flint, good balance to notching. Undamaged condition, good size, $400.00. Base corner notch, different side serrations suggest different edge use; very nice taper to blade, artistic base, $125.00. Corner notch, dovetail-related base, massive serrations for blade width, a hard worked but artistic piece, $110.00. (Private collection)

Corner notched blade, 1½" x 3⅜", from Cave-in-Rock, Illinois. Material is a glossy and high-grade flint. A well-made piece in fine condition, $100.00. (Kernaghan Collection, Colorado; Marguerite Kernaghan, photographer)

45

Thebes blades, beveled edges, 4" long. These are of white chert, ca. 6000 BC. Left: Thebes, good basal characteristics, tip damage, $50.00. Right: Thebes, damaged shoulder tip. $45.00. In both cases, the large size helps the value. (Private collection)

Adena points or blades, Mercer County flint, Ohio. Example at right is 5" long. Left: Adena, large stem for size, upthrust shouldering, $125.00. Center: Adena, unusually short stem, well-tapered blade, $100.00. Right: Adena blade, extra good size and condition, $165.00. (Gary Aeh Collection, Ohio)

Turkey-tail blade, Soshocton flint, Ohio, Woodland era. This piece has fine size at 6¼" plus is in top condition. These blades are sometimes found ceremonially broken, $135.00. (Gary Aeh Collection, Ohio)

Archaic side-notch, Ohio, 3" long. Made of very thin translucent Indiana hornstone. Basal area is heavily ground on edges, nicely balanced, good excurvate blade sides. High-quality material adds to collector appeal, $95.00. (Gary Aeh Collection, Ohio)

Exceptional blade, center example 3¾" long. Left to right: Corner-notch knife, mild irregularity to right edge outline, well-designed base, quality pale flint, $125.00. Late-Adena, translucent Flintridge, extremely thin, good design, classic type and style. Exceptional condition makes this an outstanding piece. Gem material adds value, $350.00. Archaic bifurcate, some original wear but it retains full artistic integrity. Twin-lobed knives of this size are far from common, $150.00. (Private collection)

B) The Western Midwest
(Illinois, Missouri, Wisconsin)

The ubiquitous fluted hunters moved here in about 10,000 BC, followed by lanceolate-point users. Flint and chert examples predominate, and usually the quality is quite high. If the eastern Midwest is noted for Archaic and Woodland points, the western Midwest is famed for late Paleo and Archaic specimens. Some of the finest points and blades and lanceolate styles and great numbers were made.

Archaic times, beginning about 7000 BC, brought a dependency on "modern" game animals and a more thorough exploitation of food resources. Point styles in some cases resembled those of the eastern Midwest (early Paleo forms, some Archaic blades) but distinctive types (*Dalton* forms, *Rice* varieties) were developed there or were popular in the region in early times.

The Woodland period, with pottery and plant raising, began ca. 1000 BC and the Hopewellian influence was widely felt. Their points were wide, flat and large notched, still lanceheads. Many knives were made in similar configuration. As the cultural thrust of Woodland times faded, the Mississippian town builders flourished. They were bow users.

This people arrived from the south, their main socio-religious site being Cahokia, now in the St. Louis, Missouri area. They chipped notched hoes and ovate spades from flint. Their distinctive arrowhead was the *Cahokia-notched*, with two side-notches and a single base-center notch. Triangular points were also widely used, as well as several knife forms. The usual range of chipped scrapers was present, and (as in the Southeast at the time) large ceremonial scepters and symbolic maces were made. Some "spuds," ceremonial celt axes, were chipped from flint or chert and were highly polished over the entire surface.

By about AD 1500 the ceremonial centers had declined and people like the Oneota culture came into being. They used triangular arrowheads and had many knife forms. The Oneota in turn gave way to the Missouri and Osage Indians who met and traded with Whites.

Suggested reading:

Bell, Robert E. and Gregory Perino. *Guide to the Identification of Certain American Indian Projectile Points.* Special Bulletins No. 1-4, Oklahoma Anthropological Society, 1958-1971.

Chapman, Carl H. and Eleanor F. *Indians and Archaeology of Missouri.* University of Missouri Press, Columbia, Missouri, 1972.

Struever, Stuart and Felicia A. Holton. *Koster – Americans in Search of Their Prehistoric Past.* Anchor Press/Doubleday, Garden City, New York, 1979.

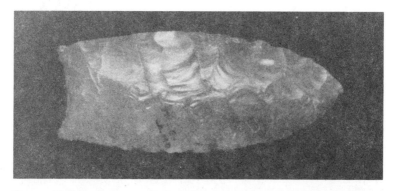

Brown Valley, Paleo period, 2½" long, made of brown-grey waxy flint. The reverse base is thinned with three short flutes. This is a well-balanced, very symmetrical piece that has outstanding workmanship and design. In perfect condition, $300.00. (Private collection, Florida)

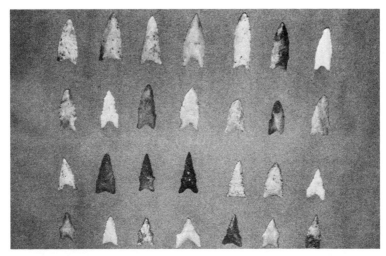

Dalton points, all from Arkansas and Missouri, very early Archaic period. Material is local flint, chert and chalcedony, and these points are from 1"-3" long. Depending on size and value factors, range here is from $35.00-$200.00. (Rodney Peck; Harrisburg, North Carolina)

Gypsum Cave, about 3" long, early Archaic, from Douglas County, Missouri. Note rounded base, flared shoulders and rapid edge taper to tip. Value: $25.00-$30.00. (Paul L. Hodges Collection, Louisiana)

Base-tang blade, probably Woodland, 2¹³⁄₁₆", glossy flint in shades of brown. A very thin and flat-faced knife. As with many prehistoric chipped blades, the two edges do not match in contour and/or degree of wear. From Pike County, Missouri, $40.00 (Private collection, Florida)

Point grouping, southwestern Midwest. Left to right: Point, corner notched, tan flint, 1¼" long. Good chipping, some damage, $4.00. Point, Archaic period, fine white flint, irregular edge line uneven base, $9.00. Blade or point, shallow side notch, glossy creamy material, no damage. A good, if unremark- able, piece, $10.00. (Private collection)

Top: point, 2¾", western Midwest, late Paleo with angled, ground basal chipping platform for basal thinning, brown chert, tip dam- age, $7.00. Bottom: late Paleo lance-olate, rechipped to a much shorter point, brown flint, good though thick for length, $15.00. (Lar Hothem Collection)

Blades or points, Missouri, longest 2", made of banded chert. Typical Archaic pieces, they are sturdy and with some basic appeal. Val- ues: $8.00-$10.00 each. (Dale Richter Collec- tion, Illinois)

Top: Graham Cave fluted, 2⅜", transitional late Paleo-early Archaic. Made of brown and grey glossy flint, both lower edges are ground, $245.00. Bot- tom: Searcy, also termed a Rice Lanceolate, 2¼" long. Made of brown semi-glossy flint, this early Archaic piece has a base that is ground and sides are heavily ground for ½", giving a stemmed appearance, $75.00. (Private collection, Florida)

Hopewell serrated blade. Left: 2¼"
x 2½", Green County, Wisconsin,
made of chert, $45.00. Right: Point
or blade, glossy chert, a well-worn
piece, $12.00. (Kernaghan Collec-
tion, Colorado; Stewart W. Kernaghan, photographer)

Points and blades, top right
point 1¾" long, all western
Midwest. Knife #752 at top is
thin for size and well made,
with straight edge bevel
chipped. Value for this 4"
piece, $25.00-$35.00. Top
row: (left to right) $17.00,
$11.00, $10.00, $25.00. Middle
row: $12.00, $6.00, $20.00,
$15.00. Bottom row: $15.00,
$15.00, $1.00, $5.00. (Richard
Warren Collection, Missouri)

Blades and points, Midwestern
states, longest piece about
3½". Left to right: Hardin, well-
barbed, white flint, $400.00.
Dalton, late Paleo, white flint,
$250.00. Dovetail, white flint,
$350.00. Hardin, white chert,
$375.00. Clovis, tan chert,
$550.00. (Ex. Sam Johnson
Collection, Arkansas)

Exceptional flint, Midwestern
states, longest piece 5½". Left
to right: Dovetail, white chert, Illinois, good size, $500.00. Dove-
tail, grey material, Indiana, well
done base, $325.00. Sedalia,
Missouri, varied colored chert,
$200.00. Adena, Missouri, white
chert, extra-long size, $375.00.
Dovetail, Illinois, white flint, fine
workstyle, $475.00. (Ex. Sam
Johnson Collection, Arkansas)

Blades and points, Midwestern states, longest piece about 4". Left to right: Hardin, barbed shoulders, white chert, Illinois, $250.00. Dalton, tan chert, Missouri, good lines, scarce type, $200.00. Snyder, Kentucky, good flint and blade size, $200.00. Adena, Beaver-tail, Missouri, Calloway County chert. This blade is both thin and well-made, $225.00. Holland, Illinois, white chert, good length, $250.00. (Ex. Sam Johnson Collection, Arkansas)

Western Midwest types (scale, top right piece 3¾" long). Left column: (top to bottom) Graham Cave blade, white flint, superior grade, $45.00. Graham Cave blade, cream flint, similar to companion piece, $30.00. Osceola blade, mottled light flint, $30.00. Scottsbluff-I (slight shouldering), reworked from longer original length, well-shaped base, $28.00. Right column: (top to bottom) Clovis, fine-grained grey flint, missing right basal corner, $40.00. Osceola, light-colored, good blade taper, $35.00. Sedalia, glossy mottled material, typical straight base, $40.00. Scottsbluff-I, tip missing, large size, $20.00. (Richard Warren Collection, Missouri)

Excellent grouping of Dickson points, with center specimen of nodular flint from Scott County, Illinois. Dickson points or blades are found in the lower Midwest and are from 500 BC into the AD centuries. Haft bases may be straight to slightly concave and shouldering is pronounced. Length of centerpiece specimen is 3⅝". Values: $75.00-$200.00 each. (Ben Thompson Collection; St. Louis, Missouri)

Searcy point, 2⅜", named for area where frequently found, Searcy County, Arkansas. It is in brown flint, stem is ground, and slight shoulders are mismatched. Ca. 4200 BC, $17.50. (Private collection)

Ultra-fine assemblage of Dalton points, all found in southeastern Missouri. They are high-grade white to tan-colored flint and average 2½" long. Longest specimen is 3". Daltons are found in the Mississippi watershed region and date from 7000-3000 BC. Note the well-serrated edges and tips common to this point type. Value range $100.00-$250.00 each. (Ben Thompson; St. Louis, Missouri)

Point grouping, several prehistoric periods. The 16 points and blades shown here are typical stream and surface finds common to the western Midwest area. Values (left to right): (top row) $4.00, $12.00, $9.00, $8.00; (second row) $4.00, $10.00, $10.00, $8.00; (third row) $6.00, $2.00, $3.00, $6.00; (bottom row) $3.00, $5.00, $4.00, $5.00. (Richard Warren Collection, Missouri)

Lanceolates, western Midwest (scale, top right piece is 4¾" long.) These points or blades are of the following types: top left, Agate Basin (?); middle right, Nebo Hill; bottom row (both), Sedalia. Values for these scarce early pieces (late Paleo/early Archaic) will range from $75.00-$125.00. Size and rarity are price factors. (Richard Warren Collection, Missouri)

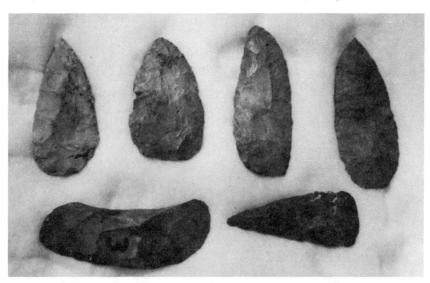

Blade grouping, Midwest. Top row: (left to right) Blade, 3½" long, pale tan chert, size the main plus, $15.00. Blade, mottled brown colors, edge-break left side, low-grade material inclusions, $10.00. Blade, semi-glossy brown flint. (As with many knives, one edge is extra-well chipped.) Uniform thickness, an acceptable blade, $45.00. Blade, semi-glossy grey chert, leaf shaped, edge retouch at tip that disturbed patina, $20.00. Bottom left: Blade, curved edge extends around both knife ends, brown and black flint, 3⅞" long. Unusual shape, $30.00. Bottom right: Blade, triangular, thick in cross section, $10.00. (Private collection)

Western Midwest artifacts, longest piece about 5". Top row: (left to right) Corner-tang knife, yellowish cream flint, Missouri. These are more commonly found in the Southern Plains region, $150.00. Ovate blade, excurvate edge, excellent size, $80.00. Middle row: (left to right) Graham Cave, well-defined base, $20.00; Hardin, speckled material, $30.00; Hardin, shoulder tip missing, fine black flint, $20.00. Table Rock, ca. 2000 BC, ground basal stem, $25.00. Bottom row: A selection of corner-notched points, all in highly collectible forms and condition. Such items typically sell from $15.00-$25.00. (Richard Warren Collection, Missouri)

Blades, western Midwest (scale, top right bi-point is 3¾" long.) Top row: (left to right) Blade, black flint, possible cache type as it was found together with piece directly below it in photo, $25.00. Blade, greatly resembling the Southern Plains Harahey, but a bit beyond normal regional distribution. A beautiful piece, $250.00. Middle row: (left to right) Blade, undamaged, sturdy and utilitarian piece, $25.00. Hardin, shoulder tip damage, good blade taper, $35.00. Bottom row: (left to right) Hardin, uneven shouldering sometimes appears with this type, $55.00. Corner-notched blade, desirable size and configuration, glossy material, $60.00. (Richard Warren Collection, Missouri)

Wadlow blades, all fine examples of prehistoric flintwork. Origin and size: (top to bottom) Marion County, Missouri, 9¼"; Madison County, Illinois, 9¾"; Lincoln County, Missouri, 10½"; Ralls County, Missouri, 11¾". Flint of such size and perfection is rarely found in modern times and this scarcity adds to its value. Such pieces are typically valued in the high hundreds of dollars. (Ben Thompson Collection; St. Louis, Missouri)

Western Midwest knives (scale, top left piece 5⅜" long.) Top row: (left to right) Tapered blade, edge beveled, quality white flint, $150.00. Paleo blade, resembles unfluted Clovis, edge worn, $110.00. Bottom row: (left to right) Ovate blade, just 5½", excellent size, extremely thin, $95.00. Squared base blade, abruptly tapered tip, glossy material, $75.00. (Richard Warren Collection, Missouri)

Dickson points and blades, western Johnson County, Missouri. In this area, the artifacts are usually made from a good type of reddish flint. Upper right example is 3" long. Dicksons began to be made ca. 500 BC. Values: (top to bottom, left to right) $20.00, $30.00, $15.00, $10.00, $20.00, $16.00, $32.50, $9.00, $2.00. (Richard Warren Collection, Missouri)

Three Archaic blades found near Forest City, Missouri in 1937. Specimen lengths: top, 9¼"; center, 10"; bottom, 8½". Material: (top to bottom) Speckled tan chert, pink chert and cream colored chert. Average value: $700.00-$1,250.00 each. (Ben Thompson Collection; St. Louis, Missouri)

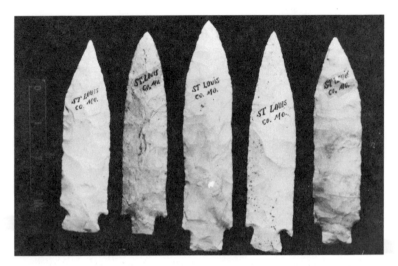

Fine grouping of Etley points or blades, all found in St. Louis County, Missouri. Note slightly different basal treatment on each of the five specimens, the overall superior workmanship, and typical blade taper near the tip. Condition is flawless and they are made from a white to tan material. Also found in Illinois, these artifacts date from the late BC years. Center specimen is over 6½" long. Average value: $700.00-$900.00 each. (Ben Thompson Collection; St. Louis, Missouri)

Fine examples of prehistoric salvage work, with the original points or blades resharpened into other useful tools. Archaic and late Paleo in origin, the rechipping produced specialized knife points, perforators or drills. These are all large artifacts, with second specimen from left, second row, 3¾" long. Average value: $125.00-250.00 each. (Ben Thompson Collection; St. Louis, Missouri)

Missouri blades with oval artifact 4⅝" long. Values (top to bottom, left to right): $4.50, $7.00, $6.00, $15.00, $2.00, $23.00. (Richard Warren Collection, Missouri)

A dozen Missouri points or blades, from Western Johnson County. Values (left to right) Top row: $4.00, $4.00, $6.00, $1.50. Middle row: $4.00, $2.00, $4.00, $2.00. Bottom row: $2.00, $10.00, $7.00, $2.00. (Richard Warren Collection, Missouri)

Point types, fine sampling of western Midwest examples, with upper right piece 3⅜" long. (Left to right) Top row: Dickson, excellent lines, good balance, $55.00; Archaic (?) era, basal and shouldering difference, $12.00; Scottsbluff (7000 BC), scarce type in good condition, $55.00. Middle row: Waubesa, late BC-early AD years, fine condition, $30.00; Dickson, slight basal irregularity, $20.00; Dickson, a beautiful type example, $45.00. Bottom row: Red Ochre (700 BC) excellent example of scarce type, $50.00; Hell Gap, (6000 BC), very good piece, representative of this uncommon early point, $70.00. (Richard Warren Collection, Missouri)

Early points/blades, all Missouri, stream and surface finds. (Left to right) Top row: Paleo form, 3¾", good grey flint, $15.00; Nebo Hill, ca. 5000 BC, lanceolate, damage between shoulder and tip, $12.00. Middle row: Afton blade, ca. 1500 BC, with diagnostic base, incurvate sides, pentagonal outline, a good piece, $65.00; Afton, with characteristics less developed or pronounced as above piece discussed, $30.00; Archaic-period blade, edge irregularities, use signs, $9.00. Bottom row: Knife, stemmed, edge outline differences, a good solid piece, $22.00; Afton (see basal comparisons), a better than average piece, $20.00; Blade (due to distance between notches), with an Archaic look, $8.00. (Richard Warren Collection, Missouri)

V. THE GREAT PLAINS
(Iowa, Minnesota, Nebraska, North Dakota, South Dakota)

Beginning about 12,000 BC, Paleo hunters came into the land with their unique killing tools, the fluted-base points followed by the Folsom people. For nearly 7,000 years they pursued large game animals, before the more measured pace of Archaic times, ca. 5000 BC. Paleo points existed in a number of forms, both fluted and unfluted. Some have been removed from in and near the skeletons of now-extinct game species, while other points have come from isolated camps and village sites.

The chipping style and skill of certain lanceolate Paleo points has never been surpassed elsewhere, and some very beautiful face patterns were made. (See Chapter XIV) As elsewhere in the U.S., the Archaic period, which lasted until about AD 500, produced a wide variety of points and blades. Most points became smaller at that time, and with either notches or stems.

In this region the bow and arrow became widely used by about AD 500, and projectile points became smaller and lighter. Many points were side notched, which allowed the jutting base corners to act as a sort of barb, increasing effectiveness when prey was struck. The many smaller cultures were the forerunners of Plains Indian tribes, eventually met by exploring Whites.

Existence for the last thousand years of prehistoric times was based on bison and small game hunting and food gathering. The Plains lifeway changed dramatically with the widespread use of the horse and firearms in the AD 1700's. They provided enhanced mobility and much greater firepower. Chipped points, for those who still used the bow, gave way to metal trade points.

Suggested reading:
Folsom, Franklin. *America's Ancient Treasures*. Rand McNally & Company, Chicago, 1974.
Steege, Louis C. and Warren W. Welsh. *Stone Artifacts of the Northwestern Plains*. Northwestern Plains Publishing Co., Colorado Springs, Colorado, 1974.

Paleo point or blade, 4" long, Cedar County, Iowa. Very good size, white quality flint, good side lines and tip. Basal fluting ½" long terminates in prominent hinge fractures at lower face center. Base corners flare outward slightly. Point thickness and slightly irregular edges do not detract from this outstanding artifact. This is an early piece with some Nebo Hill and Sedalia characteristics. $400.00 (Christopher Crew Collection, Iowa; Kirk Crew, photographer)

Arrowheads, longest ⅞", from Iowa. Left to right: Point, orange-tan flint, rounded tip is prehistoric form, $5.00. Point, misshapen, incomplete rework (?), $3.00. Point, brownish chert, Johnson Country, Iowa, $5.00. Point, grey, white and red flint, missing base corner, $4.00. (Christopher Crew Collection, Iowa; Kirk Crew, photographer)

Blade, 3" white flint with crystal inclusions, excellent beveling and serrations. Good basal balance, tip missing. From Johnson County, Iowa, $27.50. (Christopher Crew Collection, Iowa; Kirk Crew, photographer)

Obsidian point, 1½" long, very deeply side-notched, probably High Plains and Mountain area. Material is glossy black, lightly translucent, $20.00. (Private collection)

Paleo points, all from Minnesota. Top: Hell Gap-like point or blade, 8500 BC, dark chert, good form, $125.00. Bottom left: Hell Gap, balanced lines, worn chipping, $85.00. Bottom right: Hell Gap, patinated surface, basal grinding, some damage to shoulder, $35.00. (John Kolbe Collection, Minnesota; Carole Revermann, photographer)

Left: Paleo point of rusty orange Hickson quartzite, found in southcentral Minnesota. Material is from a Wisconsin quarry, $50.00. Right: Dalton point, 4000 BC, Knife River flint, from southcentral Minnesota. Note parallel double basal flutes, $15.00. (John Kolbe Collection, Minnesota; Carole Revermann, photographer)

Points and scrapers, Knife River flint, pieces found in southcentral Minnesota, glossy brown color. Large point, center row, has a value of about $15.00; less for others. (John Kolbe Collection, Minnesota; Carole Revermann, photographer)

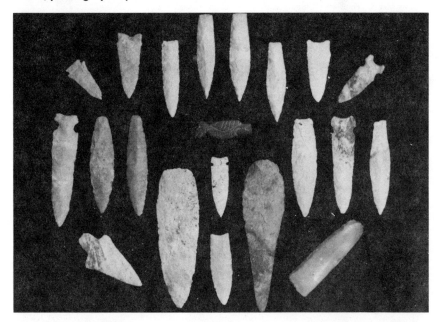

Iowa points and blades, plus small effigy (top center) and polished chipped celt (lower right). All superb specimens, value range is from $125.00-$750.00 and higher. (Old Barn Auction FindLay, Ohio)

Points or blades, longest 2⅛", Iowa. Left to right: Point, grey flint or chert, well-worked, base corner off, $6.00. Point or blade, blue flint, dark blue diagonal banding, $7.00. Point or blade, tan and white flint, balanced notches, $6.00. Paint or blade, mottled grey and white flint, thick base, $9.00. (Christopher Crew Collection, Iowa; Kirk Crew, photographer)

Blades or points, longest 3¹⁄₁₆", from Iowa. Left: excurvate sides, unusually wide for small stem, $7.00. Left center: side notch, tan flint, possibly Woodland era, $12.00. Center right: percussion-flaked side notched, brown flint, $15.00. Right: well-chipped piece in weathered white flint, black stains, $17.50. (Christopher Crew Collection, Iowa; Kirk Crew, photographer)

Points or blades, discussed in clockwise positions. Allen point, 6000 BC, made of a light grey semi-translucent Lange agate, one face covered with patina. Obliquely chipped, the Allen was named and dated in southeastern Wyoming. This example is 2½" long, $450.00. Agate Basin, 6500 BC, of chert, 3¼" long, well flaked, slightly excurvate baseline, $275.00. Fishtail Yuma, 6000 BC, of dark brown semi-translucent flint, from North Dakota. Material is known there as Knife River flint. Good lines to this piece, an uncommon find, $275.00. Agate Basin point, 6500 BC, incurvate baseline, made of chert, businesslike outline. The type was named and dated in the Agate Basin of Wyoming, $275.00. (Les Ferguson; Hot Springs, South Dakota)

VI. THE SOUTHERN PLAINS
(Colorado, Kansas, New Mexico, Oklahoma, Texas)

Sandia Cave in New Mexico's Las Huertas Canyon provided evidence that, at least in the Southern Plains, humans had chipped pre-*Clovis* points. *Sandia* points – and there is still some difference in expert opinion – seem to be from the 13-18,000 BC period. They are about 3" long, with excurvate sides, a single shoulder and varied bases depending on type.

Sandia type I points have a gently rounded base, and all edges are somewhat excurvate; they are not always as well made as type II. *Sandia II* points have a squarish base and the base bottom may be slightly or greatly concave. *Sandia III* is a modified II, having basal flutes on one or both lower faces. The fluting of type III may have developed into the Clovis technique. Here, as with all fluted-base points, basal fluting permitted a small shaft-end, thus very deep point penetration into the target animal.

The importance of Paleo points in the Southern Plains region is indicated by the number of place-names given to early points. For example, there is *Yuma* (now called *Eden* points), Colorado, and New Mexico's *Clovis* and *Folsom*, plus *Sandia*. Texas has *Plainview* and *Midland*.

The usual Paleo period lasted from about 10,000 to 5000 BC, and a range of fluted-base and later lanceolate points were made. After 5000 BC, Archaic-type peoples made a wider use of resource, with an emphasis on smaller game and wild plant foods. By the late BC years, pottery and agriculture had developed, and the bow probably arrived in the area ca. AD 500, or a bit earlier.

The region had many highly interesting and different Amerind groups. Mesa Verde, in southwestern Colorado, was the home of the cliff-dwelling Anasazi and occupation began there ca. AD 500 and lasted into AD 1300. Also known as Basket-Makers, their arrowheads were small and triangular and sometimes cane arrow shafts were used.

In late prehistoric times, many kinds of arrowheads were used, most of them notched in sime manner and a number were of gem-quality materials such as agate. Fine later arrowheads and most Paleo points are of interest to today's collector. So, too, are some Archaic pieces such as the bifurcated *Pedernales*, the single base-bottom notched *Carrizo*, the pentagonal *Afton*, and the bottom-notched *Shumla*.

With various imported "stray" points which came from all quarters of the compass, the Southern Plains collector may encounter points whose origin (style, material) may be 500 or more miles distant. Each period had a wide array of points.

Suggested reading:

Ceram, C.W. *The First American.* Harcourt Brace Jovanovich, New York City, 1971.

Parker, Wayne. *The Bridwell Site.* Crosby County Pioneer Memorial, Crosbyton, Texas, 1982.

Waldorf, D.C. and Valerie. *Flint Types of the Continental United States.* Privately published, 1976.

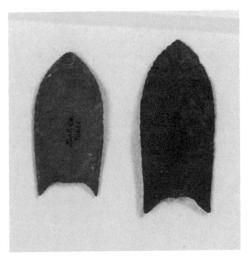

Folsom points, 7000 BC, chiefly a Western point type. Left: Folsom 2" x 1", tan flint, from Jack County, Texas. The flutes go to the tip on both sides, very thin, with typically excellent workmanship done by this herd-animal hunting people, $400.00. Right: Folsom 2⅜" x 1", dark grey flint, from Maverick County, Texas. Flutes on both faces extend to point tip. Even though these points are from the same state and general time period, the relatively simple basal outline has several visible differences, an example of small changes even in an established type. A fine point, $600.00. (Robert Hammond Collection, Alaska)

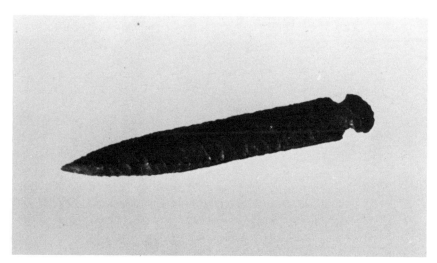

Blade, 2" x 9½", from Briscoe County, Texas. Probably an Archaic piece, it has a median ridge along each face, and the random flaking is well-done. Material is grey Edwards Plateau flint. Unusually large size adds to value, here about $800.00. (J.N. Thibault Collection, California)

Ceremonial point, from Spiro Mound, Oklahoma, 1" x 2⅛", of chalcedony. Large serrations, scarce point, $75.00. (Kernaghan Collection, Colorado; Stewart W. Kernaghan, photographer)

Castroville, center point chert, others Edward Plateau flint, from Crosby and Coryell Counties, Texas. Fairly large and attractive points, these are Archaic, ca. 4000 BC, $115.00 each. Notches begin just beyond base corners, so these are not true corner-notch points. (Wayne Parker Collection, Texas)

Texas blade and point types, 2½"-4½". Material colors are tan and grey, age-periods from 2000 BC-AD 1000. Types represented include Castroville, San Saba, Marcos, and Marshall. Values range from $75.00-$400.00 for these examples, favorites with regional collectors. (Dwain Rogers Collection, Houston, Texas)

Base-tang knives (base notched), Texas, 5"-6" long, in white, tan and grey materials. Ca. 1000 BC. Tang area is in base center, and often the notches seem almost too small for hafting a handle. Some 90% of Texas knives seem to have a definite curve to one blade edge. Size, hafting width and edge treatment and lines all indicate knife use. Examples shown range to $700.00 each. (Dwain Rogers Collection; Houston, Texas)

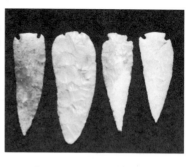

Charco points, unusual, all with one wide-barbed shoulder and single notch about halfway up opposite side-edge. These may be transitional points between lancepoint and arrowhead. Shafts found fitted into place in central Mexico were unfeathered and much thicker than arrowshafts. They are found in Texas along the Rio Grande River and into Mexico. Sizes illustrated are from 1"-2". Values are up to $60.00. Charo points are AD 1000-1500. (Dwain Rogers Collection; Houston, Texas)

Harahey knives, with the unique four-way beveled edges, average size 3½" x 4". They are found from the Texas Panhandle into the Southwest Plains and are AD 900-1300. These are mostly a west-Texas type and might be considered double-ended blades as the bevel switches at mid-blade from one side to the other. In many specimens, this did not change the outline contours, a real accomplishment. Value range is $200.00-$500.00 with more for larger examples. (Dwain Rogers Collection; Houston, Texas)

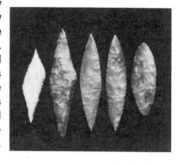

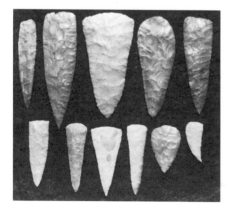

Round-base knives, 3"-7", in tan, grey and clear grey materials. Of over 4" long, most Texas blades are round or V-based. Notching or hafting greatly increases knife prices. Chipping is excellent on these examples and values range to $650.00 and beyond. Note slightly angled base-lines of the two end specimens in top row. (Dwain Rogers Collection; Houston, Texas)

Pelican Lake points or blades, from Keyes, Oklahoma, age 200 BC-AD 200. These are very well made of white or red chert, and average length is about 1½". Values: (left to right) $15.00, $30.00, $17.50. (Dale Richter, Illinois)

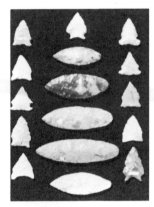

Texas point or blade types: San Patrice points, left and right colums. Top center example averages 1¼" long. They are 4000-1000 BC. This point type is usually found in Louisiana and examples shown are from $10.00-$15.00. Lerma blades or points, five examples in middle column, are dated 2000 BC-AD 1000. Some have come from early "clay mound" sites. In the Houston area, they were made from colorful river pebbles. Finer flints came from central Texas or Louisiana. Values begin at $25.00. (Dwain Rogers Collection; Houston, Texas)

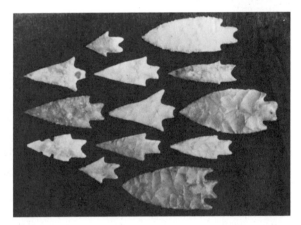

Perdernales points, or "Comanche" points, perhaps the best-known Texas point type. These examples are from 2"-5½" long, in tan, brown and light and dark grey. Bases in some are almost bifurcated and example in lower left has two additional sets of blade-edge notches – unusual. Found throughout central Texas, this is an early and longlasting type, ca. 4000 BC-AD 1000. Value range is from $45.00 (2") to $500.00 (5"). (Dwain Rogers Collection; Houston, Texas)

Side-notched blades or points, 2"
long. Left: Blade, white chert with inclusions, shallow grooved notching,
$8.00. Right: Blade, a companion
piece in bluish chert, but concave
base, $8.00. (Private collection)

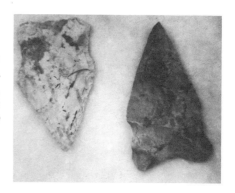

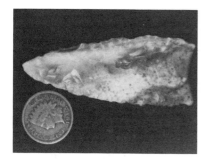

Meserve, late Paleo, 2½". Flint is a beautiful grey/brown/tan with gloss. Base
and lower sides are heavily ground and
edges have a right-hand bevel, $95.00.
From Union County, New Mexico. (Private collection, Florida)

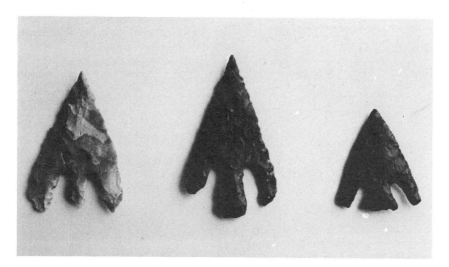

Deadman (newly named point), early Neo-Indian, ca. AD 120. Value for good
pieces: $150.00 each. Left: Edwards Plateau flint; Crosby County, Texas.
Center: Alibates flint; Randall County, Texas. Right: Petrified wood or fine
agate; Crosby County, Texas. (Wayne Parker Collection, Texas)

Points from the Southern Plains. Upper blade is 2¾" long, made of brown chert and is a very average form, $7.00. Lower left is a Paleo point made of good black flint and has excellent workmanship and design, $40.00. (Private collection)

Points, Oklahoma, some from the great mound site at Spiro. Central large point is 3½" long, of orange and white agate, from the John Day River area, Oregon. Value: $250.00. The other arrowheads are all of exceptional quality, design and condition, with many qualifying as gem-points. Their individual values are from $50.00 to an excess of $150.00 (J.N. Thibault Collection, California)

Pedernales points or blades, extra-fine condition, from 2¾"-3½". They are 4000 BC-AD 1000 and made of grey Edwards Plateau flint. They are from Brooks County, Texas. Left to right: $65.00, $75.00, $90.00, $80.00 and $70.00. (J.N. Thibault Collection, California)

Montell blades or points, 2"-4", central Texas west to the Pecos River area. Distinguished by the deep V-notch in base, they are uncommon in any area and complete examples are rare. Note the delicate, narrowed tip on four examples. value range is from $45.00 (2") to $150.00 (4") if in fine condition. The base design is one of the most memorable for the Southern Plains region. They are 2000 BC-AD 1000. (Dwain Rogers Collection; Houston, Texas)

Artifacts from Southern Plains region. Top to bottom: Point, triangular, 1½" long, $5.00. Drill section, roughly chipped, base missing, $8.00. Point, possibly Meserve-related, base and side damage, missing tip, $8.00. (Private collection)

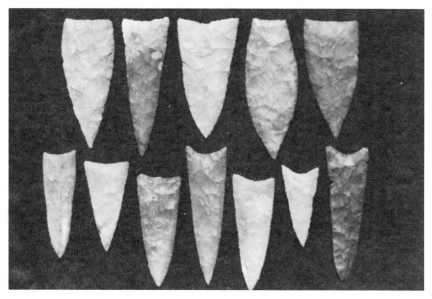

V-back blades or points, assorted ages, 2½"-4½ long. Materials are grey, clear-grey, tan and black. Values are up to $225.00 for the average piece here, much higher for examples such as bottom center which is superior in size, symmetry, workstyle and material. Some forms, such as second from right, top row, may be Paleo. (Dwain Rogers Collection, Texas)

Point group, Plains states, early types. Left to right: Point of pinkish flint, 2¼" long, serrated, minor tip damage to one basal ear, nicely balanced, $20.00. Point, possible Frio (2500 BC) with basal extensions broken, made of grey chert, $8.00. Point or blade, probably Dalton-related, one basal ear broken, yellow-white flint, $10.00. (Private collection)

Blades, Texas, various materials. Top to bottom: Tang knife, 2¼" x 4", dark grey flint, Bell County, $700.00. Tang knife, 5", light grey flint, McCollough County, $675.00. Curved knife, 5⅞", dark grey with light grey inclusions, Comanche County, $650.00 (J.N. Thibault Collection, California)

Lake Mohave, Edward Plateau flint, Crosby County, Texas. Value is $125.00 each. They are Paleo period, 7000-5000 BC. This is one of the very few points with stems longer than the upper point portion. (Wayne Parker Collection, Texas)

Garza, with single notch at base center. These are $135.00 points, true arrowheads from the late Neo-Indian times, ca. AD 1500-1665. These examples of Edwards Plateau flint are very well made. Right example is perfectly balanced. Left point is delicately serrated. (Wayne Parker Collection, Texas)

Lange, ca. 4000 BC, well-stemmed points, Edwards Plateau flint. Value: $85.00 for perfect specimens. Left: Nolan County, Texas; narrow example. Center: Val Verde, Texas; very well formed, fine chipping. Right: Crosby County, Texas; somewhat flared shoulders. (Wayne Parker Collection, Texas)

Plainview, ca. 7000 BC, with complete examples, $750.00 each. Left to right: Plainview, Tecovas Jasper, Crosby County, Texas; Golondrina Plainview, Alibates flint, Dickens County, Texas; Plainview, Edwards Plateau, Terry County, Texas. (Wayne Parker Collection, Texas)

Meserve (possibly reworked Daltons). Left and center: Edwards Plateau flint. Right: Alibates flint. These examples are from Crosby County, Texas and are late Paleo, 7000-4000 BC, with diagnostic incurvate baseline. Values: $100.00-$130.00 each. (Wayne Parker Collection, Texas)

Hell Gap, all of Edward Plateau flint, from Crosby County, Texas. Values average $95.00 each. Points are Paleo, ca. 6000 BC. They have the typical narrow base/stem, high shouldering, and rounded edges. (Wayne Parker Collection, Texas)

Clovis, early Paleo 12,000 BC. Perfect condition points are about $700.00 each. These examples (left to right) are from Comanche, Dawson and Crosby Counties, Texas. Note basal fluting on all examples and the clean, artistic lines. (Wayne Parker Collection, Texas)

Langtry, Edwards Plateau flint, Val Verde County, Texas. These average $85.00 per point and are late Archaic. Note unusual flared stem corners, concave basal characteristics. (Wayne Parker Collection, Texas)

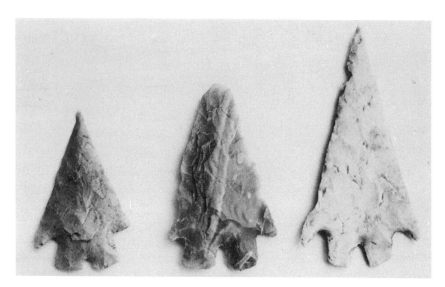

Montell, Mason County, Texas, Archaic period ca. 3000 BC. Points average $95.00 each. Left: Edwards Plateau flint, shallow bifurcate base. Center: Petrified wood, striated colors, edge wear. Right: Edward Plateau flint, good size and lines.

Perdiz, Edward Plateau flint, Crosby County, Texas. Essentially these are stemmed and barbed arrowheads. Average value: $60.00 each. They are ca. AD 1000-1500. (Wayne Parker Collection, Texas)

Bell (recently named) with similarities to Calf Creek points. Note unusual tips on 3 of 4 examples and shoulder much longer than the other. Possibly highly specialized knives, these are $175.00 examples due to unusual design, rarity and workmanship. These are early Archaic, 6000 BC from Crosby County, Texas. (Wayne Parker Collection, Texas)

Frio, long and narrow, bifurcated bases, late Archaic, ca. 3000 BC. Very attractive points with center piece of petrified wood. Average value: $175.00 each. They are from (left to right) Lampasas, Dawson and Crosby Counties, Texas. (Wayne Parker Collection, Texas)

Ensor, all of Edward Plateau flint, late Archaic. These are $90.00 points with balanced notching, fair size. Chipping is very well done, giving points an excellent finish. (Wayne Parker Collection, Texas)

Edgewood, Crosby County, Texas, late Archaic. Points are $60.00 specimens when perfect. Center example is made of petrified wood. (Wayne Parker Collection, Texas)

Abasolo, chert material, Archaic, ca. 3000 BC. These are $30.00 points, from Zapata County, Texas. Basically triangular with strong edges, bottom line tends to be gently excurvate. (Wayne Parker Collection, Texas)

Tortugas, chert, all from Zapata County, Texas. They are Archaic, 4000 BC, early simplified dartpoints, each valued at $30.00. Note efforts at basal thinning. (Wayne Parker Collection, Texas)

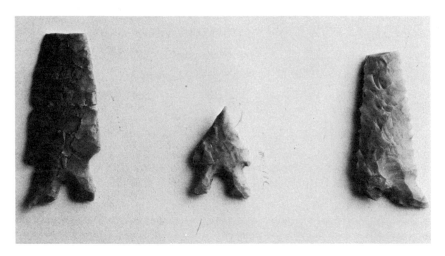

Lott, Edwards Plateau flint, medium-size and complete points valued at $85.00. Unusual regional type with bold bifurcated base. From late Neo-Indian period, they are perhaps AD 1500-1665 and may be restricted to the South Plains of Texas only. They are associated with the Garza occupation. (Wayne Parker Collection, Texas)

Harrell, all Edwards Plateau, Crosby County, Texas. These are $85.00 points, average, and Neo-Indian, AD 1100-1600, true arrowheads. Note small purpose made token notch on right point, right side, one-fifth way from tip to base. The purpose is unknown. (Wayne Parker Collection, Texas)

Washita, side-notched arrowheads, ca. AD 1200-1600. Due to amount of workmanship and fine design, these are $60.00 points. Note relatively high position of side notches on two examples (compared with other points). Left to right: Edwards Plateau flint, Crosby County, Texas; Tecovas Jasper, Crosby County, Texas; Alibates flint, Yoakum County, Texas. (Wayne Parker Collection, Texas)

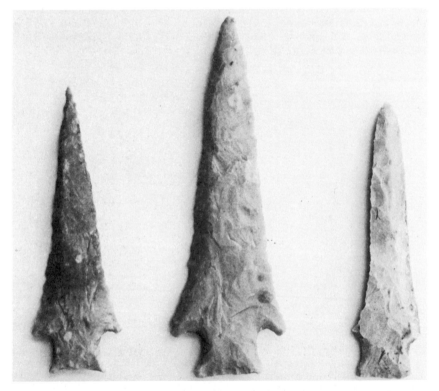

Darl, points or blades, all Edwards Plateau flint, from Comanche County, Texas. These $200.00 points are long and slender with beveled edges. They are late Archaic, ca. BC-0-AD and later. (Wayne Parker Collection, Texas)

Bonham, all Edwards Plateau flint, from Hunt County, Texas. Good specimens are about $60.00, Neo-Indian and AD 800-1200. Left: small size with expanding stem. Center: very good lines to this piece, contrasting stem. Right: serrated edge example, good length. (Wayne Parker Collection, Texas)

Marcos, Edwards Plateau flint, from Runnels County, Texas. These are Archaic, ca. 2000 BC. Value: $50.00 each, perfect condition. Note high quality of central specimen material. (Wayne Parker Collection, Texas)

Scottsbluff, Paleo, 7500-5000 BC, excellent early points. Value for complete average size points (3½" long) is $500.00. Left: River pebble chert; Lynn County, Texas. Center: Agate, classic form; Dawson County, Texas. Right: Edwards Plateau flint; Lampasas County, Texas. (Wayne Parker Collection, Texas)

Tang knives, Texas, right specimen is 3½" long. Though all are corner tang designs, note the different blade configurations on the three pieces. Left: fair blade, minor edge damage, $300.00. Center: good blade, well-curved cutting edge, $400.00. Right: fine blade, quality flint, superb condition, $500.00. (Arnold R. Logan Collection, Texas)

Tang knives. Left example is 4" long. Left: fine blade, good design and size, $450.00. Center: good blade with material change at blade corner, $375.00. Right: good blade, well-chipped, nice blade taper, $400.00. (Arnold R. Logan Collection, Texas)

Top: Marshall, 4", light-colored flint, fine condition, $250.00. Bottom: Base-notched blade (#28), dark mottled glossy flint, 4¾"; notches are unusually far apart, $400.00. (Arnold R. Logan Collection, Texas)

Texas knives, each 3½" long, various periods. Without diagnostic basal work, hafting, it is sometimes difficult to place such blades in the proper time frame. All are of exceptionally good high-gloss flint. Left: untanged corner-tanged, artistic design, good excurvate edge, $200.00. Center: blade base hinting at early hunter era, $200.00. Right: blade, very pointed tip, fine condition, $225.00. (Arnold R. Logan Collection, Texas)

Texas points and blades, various periods. Left to right: San Patrice, 1", pink quartz, $25.00. Eva, 2⅛", swirled multicolored glossy flint, $125.00. Side-notched blade or point, possible Paleo, sharply tapered at tip. A well-balanced piece, basal area very well done, in dark striated flint, $125.00. (Arnold R. Logan Collection, Texas)

Bulverde, Edwards Plateau flint, Crosby County, Texas. These are $65.00 points, from the Archaic, ca. 3000 BC. On points shown, note the stem makes up about half-point length and with flute-like basal thinning chip scars. (Wayne Parker Collection, Texas)

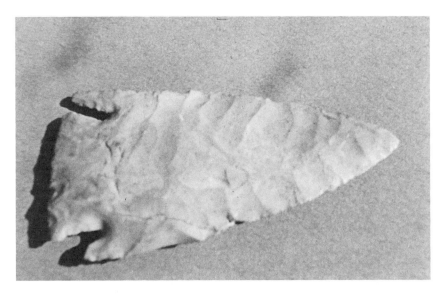

Base corner-notched blade, 2½" long, right shoulder tip missing. Large but attractive percussion scars, mottled pink flint, $75.00. (Gerald R. Riepl Collection, Kansas)

Late prehistoric artifacts, Kansas, with middle right point at 2½". All are made of the famous Alibates flint with best specimen (at top left) due to symmetry and perfection, a $75.00 piece. Others are $25.00-$50.00. (Gerald R. Riepl Collection, Kansas)

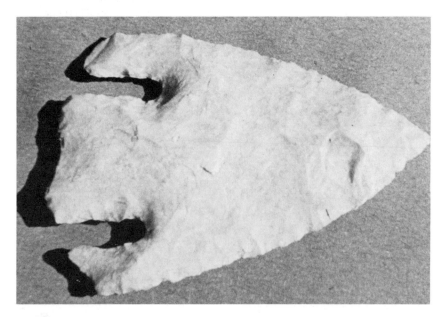

Calf Creek blade, 2¼", grey mottled flint. This is a good example of a hard-to-find point, especially with both extended shoulders matching and intact, $200.00. (Gerald R. Riepl Collection, Kansas)

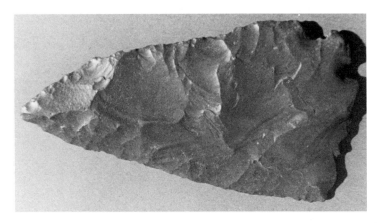

Corner-tang blade, 4", brown flint, rare for Kansas. The important working edge, opposite the tang, is in fine condition and the nonesstenial other two sides evidence percussion flaking with some pressure retouch along the top, $325.00. (Gerald R. Riepl Collection, Kansas)

Points from Paleo times, #39 is 2½" long. Right: Point is greyish chert, roughly chipped and in average condition, $8.00. Lower left: Point is cream-colored chert with some damage near tip on left side. A well-shaped early point, $12.00. (Private collection)

Ceremonial flint, 2½", notched ear and stem bottom. This may be a reworked worn-out blade, $95.00. (Arnold R. Logan Collection, Texas)

Blade, surface encrustations, unusual shape, 4¾", $65.00. (Arnold R. Logan Collection, Texas)

Plainview variant, 1⅝", quality flint, well-serrated edges, 7000-2000 BC, $95.00. (Arnold R. Logan Collection, Texas)

VII. THE NORTHWEST

(California – north of San Francisco, Idaho, Montana, northern Nevada, Oregon, Washington, Wyoming)

Points from the Northwestern states have a certain fascination to collectors of the region, this in two directions. One is the large size of certain obsidian blades, either prehistoric or those used as ceremonial objects in historic times.

Another is the outstanding beauty of Northwestern coastal and river valley gem-points. They are often small, but always made with supreme attention to workstyle and with an inspired choice of highest-grade material and workmanship.

Amerind occupation began early. Several sites on the Columbia River indicate that fishing camps existed there in 9000 BC, and Idaho's Wilson Butte Cave suggests an age of 12,500 BC. Gradually some of the interior Amerind groups moved to coastal areas and adapted to a village/seafaring lifeway. Others remained in today's Oregon and Utah and were influenced by Great Basin cultures.

There is early evidence of Paleo hunters, and the Archaic period is thought to have lasted late, in some desert areas until the coming of Whites in the AD 1700's. Most of the late prehistoric points were stemmed or notched and became smaller and lighter as the bow came into use. A wide range of point materials (see Chapter XIII) was used for chipped artifacts until they were replaced by trade goods.

As to the well-deserved reputation of excellence achieved by Northwestern points, Eugene Heflin of Oregon, in a personal communication, explains it well:

"Most states do not have the great assortment of gem-quality material to choose from that the Northwest Indians had. We have just about everything out here in gem material ... all kinds of agates, carnelian, jasp-agate, jaspers, chalcedonies, colorful cherts, even nephrite jade. With at least 32 sources of obsidian in California, six in Nevada, two in Utah, and at least 21 in Oregon – nowhere else can one find such a variety of obsidian, in at least a dozen kinds and colors."

Suggested reading:

America's Fascinating Indian Heritage. Reader's Digest Association, Inc. Pleasantville, New York and Montreal, 1978.

Drucker, Philip. *Indians of the Northwest Coast.* The Natural History Press, Garden City, New York, 1963.

Heflin, Eugene. "The Pistol River Site of SW Oregon,": *Reports of the University of California Archaeological Survey No. 67,* pp. 151-206, Dept. of Anthropology, Berkeley; July, 1966.

Indians of the Americas. The National Geographic Society, Washington, D.C., 1963.

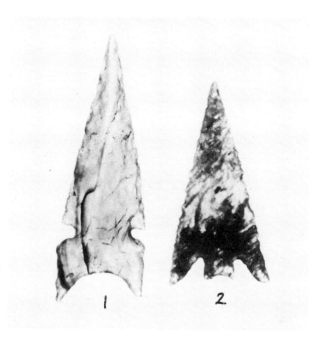

Left: Desert side-notched, 2⅛" long, from Nevada's Pyramid Lake area. Material is yellow carnelian agate with dark wavy lines. Other such points may be made of chert or obsidian. This particular type is atypical of early Desert cultures and its time period is AD 1200 to Historic times. The specimen is extremely well made, base boldly concave, condition perfect and is a well balanced piece. Value ranges are great for these points, $100.00-$600.00. Right: Gunther-barbed point, 1¾", from southern Oregon. This type ranges from Humboldt Bay, California, up to the Columbia River. Made of yellow moss agate, the material is probably from the Agate Desert not far from the Rogue. Point is likely Takelma in origin. The types are also found in Wiyot and Yurok Alagonkin cultures of northwestern California and the age is AD 900-1300. Style and material exhibit the best of the NW gem-points and value range is $100.00-$1,000.00. (Eugene Heflin Collection, Oregon)

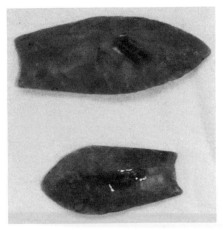

Cochise points, a variety of Clovis and of a similar early time frame. Top: Cochise 2⅝" x 1", semi-transparent chalcedony, from Eddy County, New Mexico. Scarce early point subtype and extra-fine material add to value in this case. An extra well-made point, $400.00. Bottom: Cochise, 2" x 1", semi-transparent chalcedony, from Taylor County, Texas. Good lines to this piece and high-quality material make this, and its companion piece in photo, very early forms of gem-points. $250.00. (Robert Hammond Collection, Alaska)

Rogue River points, Oregon, gem-points. Left to right: Stemmed, serrated edge, jasper, $60.00. Barb-shoulder, inclusioned jasper, $125.00. Barb-shoulder, jasper, perfect, ¾" x 1¼", $175.00. Barb-shoulder, flint, glossy, $145.00. Barb-shoulder, ultra-fine chipping, $250.00. (Kernaghan Collection, Colorado; Marguerite Kernaghan, photographer)

Points and blades, Northwestern, Black Rock Desert, northern Nevada; length ranges from 1"-1⅞". Values are about $5.00-$15.00. (E. Keith Franc Collection, California)

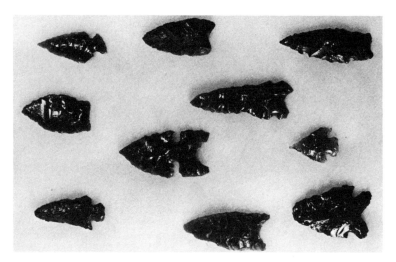

Obsidian points, Northwest, Black Rock Desert, northern Nevada, Northern Paiute Indian. (Left to right) Top row: Rose Spring corner-notch, shoulder damage, 1¼", $7.00. Black Rock concave-base, 1¼", $7.00. Humboldt concave-base, 1⅝", $10.00. Center row: (four pieces) Black Rock concave-base, 1¼", $10.00. Northern side-notch, incurvate base, 1½", $25.00. Black Rock concave-base, 1¾", $13.00. Rose Spring corner-notch, bird-point, ⅞", $12.00. Bottom row: Rose Spring corner-notch, 1¼", $10.00. Black Rock concave-base, 1½", $11.00. Elko earred, 1⅜", $15.00. (E. Keith Franc Collection, California)

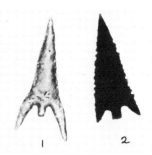

Left: Mollala or "Molly" point, 2½" long, made of gem material. The Molly point was believed by collectors to have been made by the Southern Molalla who bordered on the Upland Takelma and Klamaths and traded to these peoples, but their assumptions have not been substantiated by professional archaeologists. It is found on fishing sites of the Rogue River in southern Oregon. This one is a typical "fishing" point with long, expanding barbs, made of light yellow carnelian agate. Age is from several thousand years to White times. Points could be Shasta-Costa, Tututni, or Takelma since they are often found on these fishing sites. Prices range from $100.00-$1,000.00. Right: Gunther-barbed, serrated, 2" long of dark green translucent "bloodstone" with red spots on opaque background. Jasper was more in use on the Rogue and bloodstone is rare. Comparable in age to its companion piece in photo, this is a dramatic point with strong barbed shoulders. Typical value range is $100.00-$600.00 or whatever one will pay – but, never less. (Eugene Heflin Collection, Oregon)

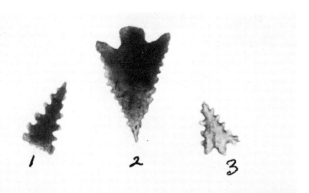

Kalapuyan points, about 2200 BC until Historic times, from Willamette Valley, Oregon. The Kalpuyas, of Penutian stock, were a nomadic people. Left: bird-point, light translucent obsidian and deep serrations persent. It is ¾" and very thin. Note how projection serrations match in number and spacing, $65.00. Center: point, 1⅛" long, very thin, of translucent obsidian. A very well-balanced and nicely serrated piece, stemmed and barbed in the classic Northwestern arrowhead and gempoint fashion, $175.00. Right: birdpoint, clear obsidian, ⅝" long, tiny contracting stem. Such small points are avidly sought by collectors. This example shows great skill in the making and even the chipping tools must have been specialized to work on such a small object, $65.00. (Eugene Heflin Collection, Oregon)

Points and blades, Northwest, Smoke Creek Desert, northern Nevada, Paiute Indian. Size ranges from ¾"-2¹/₁₆". Point types are Black Rock concave-base, Rose Spring contracting-stem, Desert side-notched, Rose Spring corner-notched, and Humboldt concave-base. Values are from $5.00-$30.00. (E. Keith Franc Collection, California)

Blades and drills, Northwest, northern California, Pomo Indian and coastal mountain groups; all obsidian. Size range for these points is 1⅞"-2⅝", values from $12.00-$40.00. (E. Keith Franc Collection, California)

Obsidian points and blades, northern California's Yolo County. Points, AD 1600-1860, $10.00-$95.00, average $40.00. Blade, 2" x 8", a ceremonial piece with value range from $650.00-$1000.00. (J.N. Thibault Collection, California)

Gunther-barbed point 2" long, with serrations from tip to barbs. It has long expanding barbs and stem. From southern Oregon, it is made of smoky translucent chalcedony with spots of green and brown. A great deal of intricate work created this beauty, and fine material adds to attraction. Points like this may sell in the $150.00-$350.00 range. It depends on the individual. (Eugene Heflin Collection, Oregon)

Obsidian points, southern Oregon, ½"-3" long. Note the wide range of sizes and styles for chipped artifacts from this region, many of gem quality. Values range from $20.00-$35.00 for smallest to $85.00-$150.00 for larger points. (Cliff Morris Collection, California; photo by Ray Pace Associates)

Points, Northwestern, from Honey Lake area of northeastern California. Top row: (left to right) Eastgate, obsidian, 1¼", $25.00. Rose Spring corner-notch, obsidian, 1", $8.00. Humboldt concave-base, obsidian, 1⅛", $9.00. Desert corner-notch, obsidian, 1¼", $16.00. Middle row: (left to right) Drill, light colored chert, 2⅛", $35.00. Rose Spring corner-notch, obsidian, ⅞", $10.00. Bottom row: (left to right) Northern side-notch, basalt, 1⅝", $9.00. Rose Spring corner-notch, obsidian, ¹³⁄₁₆", $7.00. Humboldt concave-base, obsidian, 1⅛", $7.00. Rose Spring corner-notch, obsidian, 1⅛", $9.00. (E. Keith Franc Collection, California)

Points and blades, Northwestern, from California coastal mountains, Marin County, Miwok Indians. Shortest piece is ⅞"; longest is 3¼". Value range: $7.00-$25.00 with long blade at $60.00. (E. Keith Franc Collection, California)

Points and blade, Sonoma County, California, Pomo and coastal mountain Indian groups. All obsidian, bottom right point value about $30.00. The knife blade, 3¾", is $65.00; remaining points, $10.00-$20.00 each. (E. Keith Franc Collection, California)

Blades, Northern Paiute or earlier, Black Rock Desert, northern Nevada. Top right: Concave-base blade, 2⅝", red chert, $30.00. Upper center: Side-notched blade, 2¾", brown chert, $50.00. Lower left: Stemmed blade, 2¾", red and white chert, $30.00. (E. Keith Franc Collection, California)

Northwestern points and blades, from central Nevada dry lake beds, Northern Paiute Indian. (Left to right) Top row: Humboldt concave-base, obsidian, 1½", $15.00. Rose Sprint corner-notch, obsidian, ¾", $7.00. Pinto square-shoulder, basalt, 1", $3.00. Second row: Drill or bird-point, obsidian, 1¼", $10.00. Elko earred, obsidian, excellent piece, 1½", $45.00. Third point: Rose Spring corner-notch, clear chert, 1¼", $7.50. Bottom row: Bird-point or drill, obsidian, 1¹⁄₁₆", $6.00. Desert corner-notch, basalt, 2¹⁄₁₆", $15.00. Pinto square-shoulder, obsidian, 1⅛", $10.00. (E. Keith Franc Collection, California)

Points and blades, obsidian, dry lake beds of northern Nevada, Northern Paiute Indians. Longest pieces, 2". Point types are Elko, Pinto, Desert and Rose Spring. Unusual "winged" type point in lower center is an Eastgate expanding stem, 1" long, valued at about $35.00. Other values here are from $10.00-$25.00. (E. Keith Franc Collection, California)

Points, from Black Rock Desert, Nevada, Northern Paiute Indian. (Left to right) Top row: Northern side-notch, obsidian, 1⅜", $8.00. Rose Spring corner-notch, clear chert, 1⅝", $12.00. Desert side-notch, obsidian, ¾", $20.00. Second row: Northern side-notch, green chert, 1⅜", $5.00. Northern side-notch, obsidian, 1¼", $15.00. Third row: Northern side-notch, obsidian, fine balance, ⅞", $25.00. Elko corner-notch, obsidian, 1½", $12.00. Bottom row: Drill, red chert, 1½", $11.00, Northern side-notch, obsidian, 1⅜", $8.00. (E. Keith Franc Collection, California)

Points, Northwest, from Black Rock Desert, northern Nevada, Paiute Indian. (Left to right) Top row: Elko corner-notch, obsidian, 1⅜", $11.00. Rose Spring corner-notch, white chert, 1¼", $17.00. Black Rock concave-base, obsidian, 1⅜", $10.00. Middle row: Desert side-notch, white chert, 1⅛", $25.00. Black Rock concave-base, obsidian, 1⅜", $10.00. Rose Spring corner-notch, obsidian, 1", $5.00. Bottom row: Drill, chert, 1⅞", $20.00. Single-shoulder point, obsidian, 1⅜", $17.00. Rose Spring corner-notch, obsidian, good barbs, 1¼", $20.00. (E. Keith Franc Collection, California)

Gem-blades, all Columbia River area, with largest blade 4" long. These pieces are of various high-grade materials, from different time periods. Value range is extreme, from $25.00-$200.00. (Cliff Morris Collection, California; photo by Ray Pace, Associates)

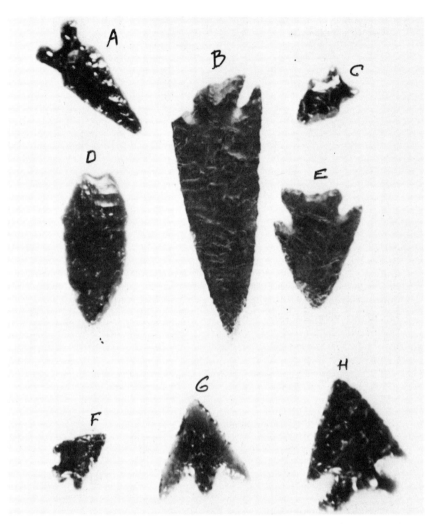

Great Basin points, all from the Oregon Desert region. A) Side-notch point, 1¼", block obsidian, $90.00. B) Corner-notch point or blade, 2½", of pitchstone, an impure obsidian. Point is extremely thin, $80.00. C) Birdpoint, ⅝", side-notched, of black obsidian, $60.00. D) Humboldt concave-base, 1⅜", obsidian, circa 650 BC. Most points of this type are longer, $50.00. E) Desert side-notch, 1½", pitchstone, concave base, 1500 BC-AD 500-600, $90.00. F) Birdpoint, ⅝", dark obsidian, corner-notched, $65.00. G) Point, 1", translucent obsidian and could be historic Bannock or Paiute. With expanding barbs and contracting stem, it has beautiful design and workstyle, $175.00. H) Elko corner-notch, 1⁵⁄₁₆", a type found in Nevada, California, and Oregon and abundant in central and western Nevada. Age: 2000 BC-AD 1080. This is a graceful point, typical of the better NW pieces, $135.00. (Eugene Heflin Collection, Oregon)

Gem-points, Columbia River area. This great river forms two-thirds of the border between Oregon and Washington state. It is a region famous for the quantity and quality of projectile points, especially of the gem types. In photo, the large center example is 2" long. Point values range from $30.00-$80.00 for the smallest and $95.00-$250.00 for the larger ones. (Cliff Morris Collection, California; photo by Ray Pace, Associates)

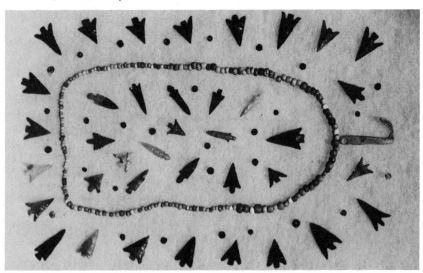

Gem-points, Columbia River area, ½"-2" long. Point types include Klickatat Dagger (slender, center), Contracting-stem, and Deschutes/Columbia points (many winged examples). Materials include agate, jasper, obsidian and quartz. Value range for such superb gem-points is $100.00-$500.00 and up. (Cliff Morris Collection, California; photo by Ray Pace, Associates)

Northwestern obsidian, including Desert side-notch, Rose Spring, Elko and Pinto point types. Size range is from ¾" (bottom right) to 2⅛" (lower left) and pieces are from the Oregon Desert, Warner Lakes area, Northern Paiute Indian. Values are in the $10.00-$45.00 range. (E. Keith Franc Collection, California)

Blades, Northwestern, from Black Rock Desert of northern Nevada. Top: Knife, 5⅜" x 1½" of blue-black chert or jasper. This is an excellent piece, good chipping, lines, edges, fine balance and in top condition. Value is about $400.00-$650.00. Bottom: Knife or lance blade made of basalt. This very early piece was found in an area with petroglyphs of mastodon. Value is mainly scientific. (E. Keith Franc Collection, California)

Northwestern points and blades, from Oregon Desert, Silver Lake area, and Northern Paiute Indian. Top row: (left to right) Pinto sloping-shoulder, obsidian, 2⅜", $45.00. Pinto square-shoulder, obsidian, 1¼", $30.00; Elko earred, obsidian, 1¼", $8.00. Center row: (left to right) Humboldt concave base, obsidian, 1¾", $35.00. Desert side-notch, obsidian, ¾", $7.00. Bottom row: (left to right) Rose Spring (?), obsidian, 1⅛", $13.00; Pinto or Elko earred, obsidian, 1¼", $16.00. (E. Keith Franc Collection, California)

VIII. THE SOUTHWEST

(Arizona, California – south of San Francisco, southern Nevada, Utah)

The prehistoric occupation pattern in the Southwest is somewhat complicated. Big-game hunters moved into some areas and did not reach others. Some Desert-Archaic people functioned successfully in certain regions, and coastal tribes had an existence by the sea. A few inland groups never left the hunting-gathering state, so the Archaic period reached well into modern times.

Point progress over the centuries was typical of many parts of North America, from large to medium to small. By perhaps 2000 BC the Cochise people grew some plants, and 2,000 years later the Mogollon, who lived in semi-underground pithouses, kept to mountainous areas.

Southern Arizona about AD 800 had the Hohokam, known for desert towns and irrigation ditches. Their points are among the finest in North America, very long, narrow and triangular. Made of fine materials, some were beautifully serrated on edges. The best were probably ceremonial in nature, used for religion or shaman's magic. Many specimens were excavated at the Snaketown site, in Pinal County, Arizona.

The Patayan and Anasazi, beginning about AD 650, combined the bow and agriculture to produce a good, basic lifeway. Confronted perhaps with climatic changes or invasions, by AD 1350 they had a serious survival problem and their traces faded. Their points were arrowheads, basically triangular, and some were corner-notched with expanding stems.

Obsidian, flint and cherts were chipped, plus some were made of rock crystal. There was a serious shortage of high-grade materials and regional supplies and imported chippable substances seem to have been treasured. One sign of this is the frequent reworking of chipped debris into small shaft-scraping tools, and the usual retipping of broken points. Of course, this was done in many parts of the country, but the practice seems widespread in the Southwest. Here, climatic conditions were sometimes harsh, except in canyons with streams or along large rivers. More than in most areas, water controlled early civilization and living areas.

Points, whether the early lanceheads or later arrowheads, seem to have met the needs of each prehistoric group, and there were a number of types and variations.

Suggested reading:

Handbook of North American Indians: SOUTHWEST. Smithsonian Institution, Vol. 9, Washington, DC, 1979.

Hothem, Lar. *North American Indian Artifacts.* Books Americana, Florence, Alabama, 1982.

Collection, Arizona, with large central blade 5½" long, in ornate old frame. There are about 142 pieces in this excellent point assemblage, ranging from Archaic to Hohokam. Some of the smaller notched examples would be considered gem-points. Value for this particular collection is in the $1,500.00-$2,500.00 range. (Dale Richter Collection, Illinois)

Pelona point, a very scarce Southwestern type, white translucent material, 1" long. Note the highly unusual diamond shape for this fine specimen, $15.00. (Private collection)

Blade or point, so corner-notched as to become stemmed, black material. From Flagstaff, Arizona, it is 4" long. This is a nicely balanced piece, $95.00. (Dale Richter Collection, Illinois)

Arrowheads, obsidian, California, 6 o'clock example 1⅛" long. Light-colored point in 8 o'clock position is an agate point from Arizona. These Southwestern gem-points are in the $20.00-$50.00 range. (Hershberger Collection, Indiana; Jeff Hershberger, photographer)

Obsidian blades and points, all California, large leaf-shaped blade 4¾". (Left to right) Top row: Stemmed blade, slightly shouldered, median ridge, $45.00. Leaf-shaped blade, perhaps a pre-form, good condition, $50.00. Corner-notched blade, outstanding workstyle and balance, excellent basal symmetry, smooth edges, $200.00. Bottom row: Wide-stemmed blade, unequal shouldering, perfect condition, $40.00. Triangular blade, $20.00. Base-notched point, irregular edging, $25.00. Wide-stemmed blade, tip damage, a sound, sturdy piece, $25.00. (Hershberger Collection, Indiana; Jeff Hershberger, photographer)

Obsidian points or blades of good size and condition, California. Top: Corner notch, slender for size, excellent chipping, $125.00. Bottom: Side notch,even edging, well-notched base, $150.00. (Hershberger Collection, Indiana; Jeff Hershberger, photographer)

Points, two stemmed and remainder side-notched, California, average length ¾". These are in the $15.00-$30.00 range. (Hershberger Collection, Indiana; Jeff Hershberger, photographer)

Points, southern California Desert and Death Valley areas, various materials and periods. Top row: (left to right) Gypsum point, chert, 1¼", $3.00. Rose Spring, obsidian, 1⅛", $4.00. Pinto square-shoulder, obsidian, 1⁵⁄₁₆", $5.00. Center row: (left to right) Desert corner-notch, chert, 2⅞", $45.00. Bottom row: (left to right) Elko corner-notch, obsidian, 1⅝", $12.00; Pinto single-shoulder, obsidian, ⅞", $9.00. Rose Spring grey chert, 1¼", $7.00. Rose Spring, chert, 1¼", $7.00. (E. Keith Franc Collection, California)

IX. CANADA

(Large provinces east to west that touch the 48 adjoining U.S. states: Quebec, Ontario, Manitoba, Saskatchewan, Alberta, British Columbia)

In prehistoric times there were of course no international boundaries, no contiguous United States or Canada. The whole region north of what is now Guatemala (the beginning of Central America) was, and is, North America. Many points common to the northern tier of the U.S. can also be found in southern Canadian areas, and vice versa. Since Amerinds came through present-day Canada to spread elsewhere, it is likely that the oldest New World human occupation dates will eventually be found in that country.

Quebec, one of the widest provinces above the U.S.-Canadian border, is a peninsula bounded by Hudson Bay, the Atlantic, and the Gulf of St. Lawrence. Northeast U.S. point types, especially those of northern New York state, are found in the lower areas of Quebec. There is a wide range of points from the Paleo and Archaic lifeways, fewer from Woodland times. Point materials are similar to those of the U.S. Northeast, plus some chert and flints native to Quebec.

Ontario, due north of the U.S. Midwest "heartland" of Amerind occupation, has some continuation of northern Midwest point types. What may be very early chipped artifacts were found near the town of Shequiandah, suggesting ages in excess of 25,000 BC. Fluted-base points resembling those of the eastern U.S. have been found in numbers in the southwestern portion of Ontario. Other early forms include the unfluted *Plainview* and the beveled-edge *Meserve*.

Manitoba, southwest of Hudson Bay and above North Dakota, had a considerable Paleo and Archaic occupation, and some points were made of U.S. flints, traded northward. The province is long and narrow, like Alberta and Saskatchewan, and northern areas lacked top-grade flints. Centered at the upper North American landmass, Manitoba has a wide range of points that came in from the east, west, and south. All early types seem to be represented, at least in small numbers.

Saskatchewan has produced fluted *Folsom* points in the southern part of the province, and the *Scottsbluff* has been found. The Rocky Mountains to the west were somewhat of a cultural barrier in early times, and other U.S. point types seem to have gone northward including the *Eden* and *Agate Basin*. Or, it may someday be proven that such points developed in Canada and the concept went southward. Saskatchewan has a number of late Paleo points, suggesting a large number of herd animals at one time.

Alberta, like the other provinces, offered a comfortable environment to early hunters, and many points are of the stemmed lanceolate design. The *Alberta* point or blade is well-known, and is also found to the south, in Montana. Archaic Indians had one point similar to the *Hardaway* of the southeastern U.S., and double-pointed *Laurel Leaf* blades are also encountered. Other points similar to those of the U.S. Northern Plains are found, including the angle-bladed *Cody* knife.

British Columbia, western-most of the lower Canadian provinces, had human habitation beginning at least by 11,000 BC at Fraser Canyon. Western British Columbia had a partial continuation of gem-point making, and obsidian and yellow rhyolite were chipped. Scottsbluff and other early points have been found plus many Archaic point types.

Suggested reading:

Wormington, H.M. and Richard Forbis. *An Introduction to the Archaeology of Alberta, Canada.* No. 11, Denver Museum of Natural History; Denver, Colorado, 1965.

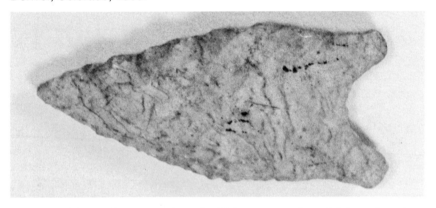

Meserve, Paleo point, approximately 2" long, an early point type found on the High Plains of Canada. These may average in age to 4500 BC and be as old as 7000 BC. This example is made from a light brown flint and is in fine condition, $95.00. (Howard Popkie; Arnprior, Ontario, Canada)

Canadian artifacts, all from Ontario, clockwise: Arrowhead, wide-shoul-dered, Algonquin, $6.00. Blade, 2¼" long, mottled flint, $5.00. Tri-notch, well-shaped, lobate corners, $16.00. Blade, wide stemmed, $15.00. Center: Arrowhead, 1¼", stemmed, rounded shoulder tips, $8.00. (Howard Popkie; Arnprior, Ontario, Canada)

Canadian points, clockwise: Lace warpoint, 2¾" long, Haida Indian from West Coast of Canada, ca. AD 800, $15.00. Lace warpoint, light flint with pink impurities, very large serrations, $10.00. Stunning point, 2" long, dark red jasper, from Jasper, Alberta. Possibly Blackfoot, AD years, $9.00. Bifurcat-ed-base point or blade, probably Archaic, $10.00. (Howard Popkie; Arnprior, Ontario, Canada)

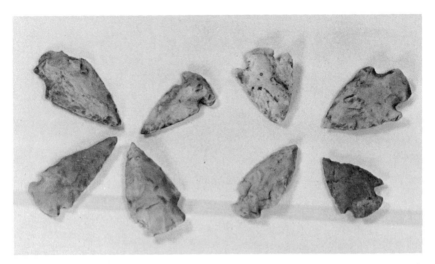

Canadian chipped art, all from the Ottawa River Drainage Basin. Length range from 1½"-2", of light brown flint. Such points were made by Huron and Algonquin ancestors, ca. AD 1000, and by the Iroquois, AD 1600. Value range for points of this quality and size is $5.00-$12.00. (Howard Popkie; Arnprior, Ontario, Canada)

Canadian arrowheads, ½"-¾" long. Clockwise: Side-notch or wide-stem, $6.00. Birdpoint, obsidian, well-serrated, found at Medicine Hat, Alberta, ca. AD 1000, $16.00. Stemmed arrowhead, good chipping, $8.00. Triple-notch point, triangular outline, $14.00. Point, concave side notches, good tip, $4.00. Triple-notch point, excurvate base, $5.00. Stemmed arrowhead, barbed shoulders, $4.00. (Howard Popkie; Arnprior, Ontario, Canada)

Canadian artifacts, all from Manitoba. Clockwise: Point, side-notch, layered flint, $8.00. Harrell arrowhead, 1", AD 1200, $14.00. Blade, tri-notch, brown flint, $13.00. Point, incurvate base, side-notched, $7.00. Blade or point, nicely side-notched, $10.00. Center: Point, large side-notches, $4.00. (Howard Popkie; Arnprior, Ontario, Canada)

Canadian points/blades. Top: (left to right) Algonguin, 2¾", AD 1000-1700. $10.00. Algonguin triple-notched, well-balanced point, $20.00. Bottom: (left to right) Beavertail, 2700 BC, $9.00. Blade, brightly banded flint, $11.00. Beavertail, wider shoulders than example shown at left, $9.00. (Howard Popkie; Arnprior, Ontario, Canada)

X. PROJECTILE POINTS –
Some Observations

In addition to the points and/or blade types presented in the eight U.S. regional divisions, there are many others of collector interest. Most of the widespread and distinctive points have been typed or named because many specimens are recognized by many people. They are the "official" points.

Often the names come from the place (*Folsom*, New Mexico; *Nebo Hill*, Missouri), site (*Frazier*, Tennessee; *Garza*, Texas), or area (*Fox Valley*, Illinois; *Cumberland*, Cumberland River Valley, Kentucky and Tennessee) at or near where they were first found. Then, the points were described and verified as being special, somehow different from all others.

It might be mentioned that a number of points that are similar have different names in different regions, or, more than one name. An example of the first is the tri-notched *Harrell* arrowhead, also known as a *Cahokia* point. An example of the second is the *Robbins* blade, also referred to in collecting circles as a late-*Adena* piece. Still others, like the lovely Archaic *Glacial Lake* points have been largely ignored in the literature.

Some points have a name (*bottle-neck, turkey-tail*) coined because part of the artifacts, the bases, reminds one of a known present-day configuration. In these two cases, imagine early pointmakers' consternation were they to know their points would be named after a container of an undreamed-of material, glass and the denuded end of America's largest game bird.

Still other points (tiny *birdpoints*, triangular *warpoints*) are so-called because of their supposed use against feathered targets and in conflict. These are now considered to be general-purpose arrowheads, efficiently designed for the times and bow-and-arrow use.

On the average, an Indian arrowhead never tipped an arrow at all. Probably fewer than one-in-ten points can be so-classed, and in some areas, it would be one-in-twenty or fewer. (Some locations, however, due to a heavy population in late times, do have more small arrowheads than other points.) The bow-and -arrow combination is thought to have arrived in North America quite late and the era 500 to 1000 AD is usually considered accurate, depending on part of the country. Arrowhead dates for the Eastern U.S. are generally later than for the West.

Since Native Americans have been here since at least 25,000 BC, most points tend to be pre-bow. Then, the chief weapons system was a light lance or javelin (not truly a spear, which is largely hand-held) propelled by an *Atl-atl,* a carefully shaped stick about 18" long. A hook at the stick end engaged the lance-butt, and the added leverage allowed the lance to be thrown harder than with the unaided arm.

The Atl-atl had a hand grip region at the base, and often a weight was attached, this made of any stone that worked well and looked good. The weights, often themselves in very artistic forms, probably served two functions, and there is not a whole lot of evidence that they were used simply to propel a lance to greater distance due to increased momentum. Added weight could more easily have been built into the stick itself.

One function was likely that of magical or decorative symbol, for the "weights" were generally far better made than they needed to be. Another function was the very practical purpose of counter-balancing the lance with chipped point. The lance, with tip and wooden shaft that was 4½' to 6½' long, probably had to be held in a horizontal position before an accurate aim and cast could be made.

However held and used, the lance thrower and lance point held sway in North America for at least 10,000 years. Some scientists think the early Paleo people had it 15,000 and more years ago. The bow never did entirely replace the lance thrower, and the device remained in use into historic times. This was so with such people as Alaskan Eskimos and in Meso-American, even in the American Southwest. *Atl-atl* is a Mexican-Indian (Aztec) word and their name for the device. Wherever used, it magnified throwing force some 50 to 65 percent.

The lance persisted in use because most prehistoric cultures were slow to make changes and innovations. But the bow replaced the *Atl-atl* and the lance was replaced by the arrow, this likely for several reasons, all of them important in prehistoric times. The bow was faster and more accurate and it had a greater range, though sheer striking power was less. Since arrowheads were much smaller, more could be chipped from the same amount of raw material. Arrowshafts were much easier to make than lanceshafts and more could be carried on the hunt. Finally, the bow and arrow had less size and bulk, was at least as effective as the lance, and was far more convenient. Not surprisingly, there is evidence of increased inter-Indian warfare accompanying the spread of bow use.

With lances in use about ten times as long as bow, the average projectile point is often a lancepoint. Even without knowing the approximate age of a point, design features often help clue the collector to the original purpose. Arrowheads were configured to the ¼" arrowshaft, not the ½" (average) lanceshaft diameter.

Arrowheads tend to be fairly lightweight, have a narrow hafting area and even if long, they are comparatively thin. Given their vast time span and greater numbers, lanceheads exist in many more types and styles. They tend to be heavier, wider and longer than arrowpoints, often thicker as well. All this is *generally* true, but there are exceptions. These were caused mainly by something called a foreshaft.

The lance itself, which may have been feather-vaned for increased accuracy, in some cases had a much smaller bone or wood shaft set in the tip end. The point was thus fastened to this smaller shaft, not the larger main lance body. This would have remained in the target animal, allowing the valuable main shaft to fall away and be reused. A new foreshaft was inserted, and the weapon was again ready. To tip the foreshaft, which had a diameter of ¼" to ⅜", a much smaller point could be used. This perhaps was the reason for such tiny Archaic points as the Lake Erie Bifurcated point, often about an inch long, and with base sometimes less than ½" wide. Such small size usually means an arrowhead, but not always.

Even with lancepoints, a very large number actually were knives, this indicated by design features or signs of actual use. To complicate matters even more, some points served that purpose, and then doubled as knives as well. No one statement of original use or purpose can be absolutely correct for any one type.

While there are many hundred point types, there is one point that can be found almost anywhere. Canada, the 48 adjoining states, Mexico, Alaska, no matter – the point turns up with some regularity. A top collector piece, it is the famous fluted-base Clovis, and all forms are basically the same.

Used to hunt animals now long-extinct, the Clovis (with a number of variants) may be 12,000 years of age. They are preferred for size, averaging 3", graceful channel fluting, good material, flowing contours and expert overall flint-working. Clovis points were made with skill and precision, as fine tools always are.

The only other chipped artifact to be nearly as widely distributed is the end-scraper, from ¾" to 2" long. The beveled scraping edge, curved, was located on one end of the large flake. Very sturdy, it was used to scrape tallow and fat from hides and skins, a vital step in curing such animal coverings.

In true importance to the Amerind lifeway, the omni-present scrapers have long been ignored by most collectors, and their artistic merit has been largely overlooked. Still, the scraper was as much a survival tool as the more exciting points and any collection should have some examples.

Consider that a hundred years from now, collectors will be amused that we only acknowledged some 4000 or so point types, for 21st century collectors will have two and three times that number to study. A competent futurologist familiar with the point field would have much fun projecting just two aspects of it. One would be point values, with a huge number of persons competing for a non-increasing resource. Another would be points recognized and widely accepted as real prehistoric artworks. This last would be a tribute both to collectors, the people who knew it all along, and to the ancient artisans. They did what they could and knew it was good.

Point comparisons: Though both are about the same length, 1" (left) and 1¼" (right), perhaps 6,000 years separate the two. Early knappers chipped as well as, and in some cases better than, later Amerind peoples. Left: Arrowhead, side-notched, irregular baseline, AD 1000, $8.00. Right: Lancehead, bifurcated, ca. 5000 BC. Base lobe-ends are fracture-chipped flat, $25.00. (Private collection)

Point type group, various regions. Clockwise: Fish-spear (outline somewhat resembles a fish), dark flint, $7.00. Godar, 2½", good outline, made of inferior chalk-like chert, $11.00. Hardaway, mottled blue and grey chert. Not a common point type, $18.00. Carrollton, long-stemmed, crudely worked, $4.00. (Private collection)

#115: Godar, 2", good lines, low-grade material, $10.00. Left: Hafted flake, scraper form. The "profile" on right edge is probably unintentional. Scrapers like these have little monetary value. #117: Unknown blade, base-fluted for two thirds obverse length, late Paleo or early Archaic, $18.00. (Private collection)

XI. ARTIFACTS MADE FROM POINTS

Amerind point makers and users were generally frugal when it came to their chipped art. Tools were used and reused constantly, since it was apparently easier to re-tip a point or re-edge a blade than create a new artifact. All this evidence is in the hands of collectors who have done an excellent job of preserving such prehistoric works.

Points tended to be broken in use and made shorter. Many examples have the normal-size base and less-than-average length. Collectors still consider them on existing merits, not what the point once was or might have been.

The same applies to knives. Rechipping usually kept the base or haft area intact and in size, while blade length may have decreased. Almost always, the blade became narrower as dull edges were removed in the resharpening process. Some examples were so worn-out for knife use that they became, like some points, utterly different tools.

With hafting structures so usable, short and narrow tips were probably used as perforators, holing wood and leather, or were used as a type of awl or needle. Still other points became so narrow that they were chipped into drills. These – whatever the basal design – had a relatively long and narrow projection that was about as thick as wide, with or without use-polish on the shaft sides.

Today's collector tends to put broken points in the "keeper" box, considering them not worth displaying, but worth more than being thrown away. Amerind users had a related problem, in that the points, when broken, no longer served the original purpose. But instead of being discarded, many were made into scrapers.

Scrapers made from points are collected as authentic Indian artifacts, but they do not have much value, even when the example is well made. (Evidently, collectors can identify more with a point used to kill a deer, than with a scraping utensil used to dress that deer hide.) Termed "hafted" scrapers because they still have the original notching or stemming, the broken point became another tool.

Chipping at the break area, a new edge was formed in one of two areas. The more common was to chip so that the slightly excurvate new edges were flush with one face. The chip line was always done from one side, making a scraper edge that was beveled and very strong for rough use. Another scraper design was to chip from both sides, which moved the scraping edge to the blade center, a straight line between the two original point edges. Possibly part of the shaft was used as a handle, or a new and shorter one was made.

Background aside, some scrapers have some value as collectible art. These are hafted scrapers and scrapers of very fine basal design and chipping. Scrapers made of a near-gem material will retain some value because of inherent material worth. But overall, most collectors seem to feel the scrapers, no matter how attractive, never lose the stigma of being incomplete points.

Point bases were also used to become two other classes of artifacts. Sometimes the break area was fracture-chipped in a novel fashion, not across the break, but down, toward the base. Usually done on the edges, but sometimes on the face as well, the sliver-chipping process left sharp edges and small tips. These were tremendously strong for size, being backed by point bulk, and were probably used to cut bone or antler.

Most people know that Amerinds worked flint by chipping. What is not generally known is that flint was also shaped by abrasion, by rubbing the object against a flat, loose-grained stone, wearing the flint away. Sometimes seen on portions of worked loose flakes, an artifact class was also made. These are point bases that had the break area ground smooth. Usually the surface is angled more toward one face, giving a single working edge, but sometimes it was flat-ground, giving two edges. Many collectors pass these tools up, perhaps only wondering why the break area is so flat. This was not accidental. The tools could be termed "ground-edge shapers" and their purpose was probably to work wood, being a sort of miniature chisel.

While point bases were generally utilized, the tip and tip-sides were not overlooked. Occasionally collectors find an Archaic period point with one side fluted, the handiwork of earlier Paleo people or a broken point from times before was reworked into a later arrowhead.

Salvage was a common prehistoric practice and some strange, seemingly impossible, combinations can turn up. This is just one aspect that makes point collecting such a fascinating field.

Ground-edge shapers, described in chapter text. Center example is over 3" long. As photo indicates, the break area was ground flat or slightly angled and there is use polish along the working edges. With bases present, it is easy to identify the point types, which are as follows: (left to right) Bottleneck (Archaic), Meadowood (Archaic), Adena (Woodland). There are no established values for these unusual tools. (Private collection)

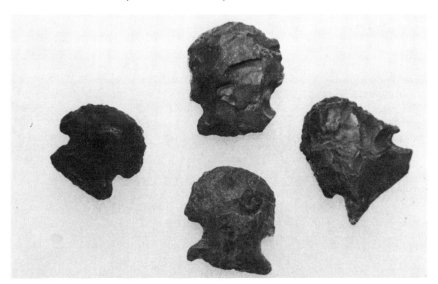

Hafted scrapers, excurvate edge opposite notching is the working portion. Very often these notched scrapers are made from points or blades and are usually 1"-2" long. Such examples are valued in the $5.00-$11.00 range. One advantage of collecting these pieces is that they are not faked in numbers. These examples are from Lycoming County, Pennsylvania. (Gary Fogelman Collection, Pennsylvania)

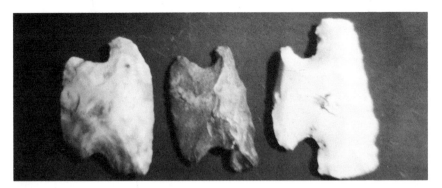

Hafted scrapers, averaging ⅝" long, 1" wide. Made from projectile points that were broken, these are common in many collections. Values for these are in the $3.00-$5.00 range. (Private collection)

Resalvaged points, 1"-1¼" long, respectively. While these may not appear to be unusual, they are fine examples of material utilization by later Amerinds. Both are old pieces, made into arrowheads. Left: The broken tip of an Archaic beveled blade was rechipped into a triangular arrowhead with excurvate base. Right: Another Archaic point had stem rechipped and shoulders reshaped to produce an unnotched arrowpoint. Values depend on how interesting each rework is to a particular collector, but dollar worth would not be high. (Lar Hothem Collection)

Points eastern Midwest, about 1" long. They are of interest because of the highly unusual edge serrations. Due to the distance between serrations, they are more of an edge-notched type. These may be projectile points or specialized tools. Values: $15.00-$25.00 each. (BLH Collection)

XII. OTHER CHIPPED ARTIFACTS

In prehistoric and historic times, many artifacts other than projectile points were chipped. Some two dozen additional classes are listed here and all have some degree of collector appeal.

Axes: Large chopping artifacts, they are often poorly made of low-grade material. There is often crude notching for a handle. The axes are usually surface finds throughout much of the country. Some collectors believe they are very early, though some examples may simply be poorly made, from later times. Most axes are roughly percussion-flaked and blade edge is never ground or polished.

Blades: Most hafted large flint pieces can be assigned a time frame due to basal configuration and other factors. "Blades" here means chipped artifacts that were almost certainly used as knives, but the blade form provides no convincing clues to exact origin. These are the types that do not resemble large points but may have dozens of other forms.

Burins: The word (perhaps the French *burino*) means an engraving tool, but Amerind burins were for more than making marks. Formed by fracture-chipping a flake edge, this created small, very strong and sharp tips. These could be used to score antler and bone in preparation for breaking, and so form other tools. Some burins are thought to be very early.

Celts: These are axes without notches or grooves and a single blade opposite a rounded poll. A supposedly early type was crudely percussion flaked. A later type from the Mississippi Valley was a true work of art and had the blade and body areas highly polished.

Chisels: Again thought to be late in prehistoric times, chisels have a long, narrow body and very narrow cutting edge, usually polished. Though most were made of hard stone, some were chipped in flint. The rare chipped adz was similar to the axe, but with a curved cutting edge.

Choppers: This is a very general class and many kinds of large chipped artifacts could claim membership. Whether crude or well made, most seem to be hand-held with a large general-purpose edge. Materials range from very poor to gem-quality.

Cores: These are the material platforms, the "parent block," from which were struck bladelets and scraper-spalls. If enough mass remains, and material and color are good, there is a certain amount of collector interest.

Drills: Long and slender, drills are a favorite collector item. Most are artistic and well made. Drills in unbroken condition are not common, and values for better pieces can be high. Not all chipped drills were used with circular motion to make holes. Some were probably hairpins; others punched hides or skins in preparation for sewing. When obviously purpose-made for the task and not just a worn-down point of blade put to a different purpose, drills have a distinctive beauty of their own.

Flake tools: One of the great prehistoric technologies was the skill of striking off a useful piece of flint, either by direct or indirect percussion. Bladelets, long and slender, were tools in themselves. Other fan-shaped chips became scrapers. Even large chips from the point manufacturing process were sometimes reworked and used as small blades or scrapers.

Gravers: These are worked flakes with one or more short, sturdy tips. The tips would have been useful for many marking and engraving tasks. Some graver tips or spurs were placed at one corner of an end-scraper, a frequent practice in Paleo times.

Gun-flints: The ultimate weapon of early historic times was the muzzle-loading musket which used a flint-lock firing mechanism. Most of the firing flints or gun-spalls were acquired via international trade, and many were made in England and France. Native Amerinds also manufactured the flints. For example, many gun flints were found at the AD 1700's Guebert site in Illinois. At least 25% of recovered examples were of Indian origin, either totally Indian-made or reworked European flints.

Hammerstones: Flint balls for pounding are not common, for they were apparently quite difficult to shape. Once made, however, the extreme hardness of the material made them very durable. Most exist in diameters of over 1" to under 4".

Hoes: Late-prehistoric hoes were used by agricultural societies and the wide, flat pieces sometimes have hafting notches. Chipped hoes sometimes have a highly polished blade area largely due to in-use wear. Some examples approach workstyle that is ceremonial grade.

Knives: (Also see *Blades.*) Knives were made in at least 18 forms and were artifacts designed only for cutting or scraping. Some were casually made "throwaway" pieces, while others evidence great care in the making.

Perforators: Often a longish tip on a medium or large flake, perforators do not have the strength of gravers nor the length of most drills. Many have a sharply tapering tip. They were apparently used to punch holes in hides or skins. As a matter of curiosity and speculation, some perforators are so small they may have been used as tattooing needles. Perforators are sometimes called "punches."

Reamers: Drill-like, these tend to be much longer and larger with wide bases. Reamers may have been used to enlarge or further shape drill holes.

Saws: For the most part, chipped saws were not part of the Amerind tool kit. Serrated edges are found in profusion, but most seem too small or short to serve a serious sawing function. It is thought that saw-tooth edges were mainly knife features.

Scrapers: Scrapers are found all across North America and were made by all cultures. Features include great size ranges and material differences, plus location and size of the scraping edge. Some are of hand-held dimensions while others were probably mounted at right angles on a short, sturdy handle. Most edges were somewhat small and with bevel-chipping so that great pressure could be applied to a relatively small area.

Shaft-scrapers: Purpose-made artifacts chipped from a large flake, most examples have basal notches for a handle. From 1" to 4" long, the main working edge is concave, steeply beveled and usually on the left side of the scraper. Another small edge is usually present elsewhere on the scraper, evidently for finer work. It is thought that these objects were used to shape lanceshafts.

Shaft-smoothers: Often these are thin chips with sharp edges, into which are worn one or more concave depressions. These show the edge-polish produced by constant contact with hardwood. Depending on the actual purpose, these half-moon shaped depressions are from ¼" to 1" across, of varying depths, but usually shallow.

Spades: Like hoes also mainly from later times, chipped spades tend to be larger and longer than hoes and more sturdily made. Some are notched at the base, while others are elongated. The base is usually more narrow than the digging end.

Spears: "Indian spearpoint" is a frequent description for large point-like chipped artifacts. Except for certain regions and special occasions, there does not seem to be widespread spear use in prehistoric times. Most "spears" appear to have one or more knife characteristics.

Spokehaves: This is not a well-defined tool but most seem to have a concave chipped-in edge. Hand-held or handled, a large number indicate that woodworking and shaft shaping were quite important. Sometimes spokeshaves were combined with other tools. In Texas, they were occasionally chipped into drill bases. Elsewhere, they have been found on point base bottoms. A related artifact is the larger rectangular chipped blade, the drawshave with evidence of hafting at each end that suggests two handles.

Spuds: This is a misleading term and it is derived from a tool used by Whites to dig potatoes in historic times. These are generally Mississippian-era ceremonial objects, very occasionally chipped in flint and polished until chip marks disappeared.

Flint hand-size chopper, working edge to left, made of a rough grey chert. This piece is 5½" long. While there is little evidence to support the view, most collectors feel these are very old artifacts. (Lar Hothem photo)

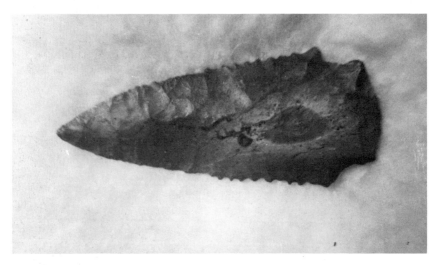

Archaic blade, wide-stemmed, made of Harrison County (Indiana) flint, in several shades of grey. This flint is nodular, and nodule center can be seen between the shoulders of this piece. Edge-line on both sides has a light and pleasing gentle twist, unusual. This example is 3" long, $90.00. (Private collection)

Cache blades, 6"-6½" long. Such ovate specimens are sometimes found in large numbers, either as "accidental" deposits or as ceremonial inclusions in special sites, often mounds. Cache blades have a certain mystical attraction for most collectors. Though many are rough-chipped, these examples (late pre- historic) might be valued at $30.00-$75.00. (Joseph D. Love Collection, Tennessee)

Drill, 2⅛" long, good taper, very fine chipping and edge retouch, creamy semi-translucent Flintridge, $50.00. (Lar Hothem Collection)

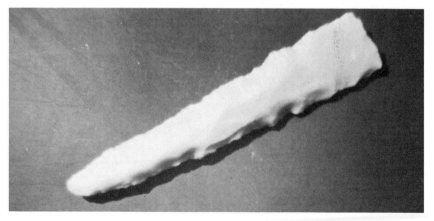

Drill, 2⅝"long, translucent pale grey Flintridge. This is a finely made piece, good size and shape, flattened top, $70.00. (Private collection)

Hafted shaft-scraper, 1⅞" long, ca. mid-Archaic for eastern Midwest. Made of a quality brown and cream flint, it is thought the curved and beveled edge to left was used to shape lance shafts and similar woodworking. Classic form, $50.00. (Private collection)

Charmstone, 2" at greatest length. This is a quality black flint with swirls of brown color, a large flake with all edges chipped (not a scraper) and polished and both faces polished. Probably an item from a shaman's pouch or sacred bundle, use and purpose unknown. No value can be determined for such one-of-a-kind pieces. (Sue Hothem Collection)

Drill, 2⅜", of unknown glossy blue and grey flint. Drillshaft has use-polish on all sides. A well-shaped piece of better than average length for type, $70.00. (Sue Hothem Collection)

Gunflints, of the type often picked up on historic Indian sites. These were used to strike firing-sparks for flintlock rifles and muskets. Center example is about 1" square. Though some were chipped by Indians, many were European imports and were used by Whites and Indians alike. Value range is from $10.00-$15.00. (Private collection)

Drills, reamers and perforators, all Missouri finds, with top example 5½" long. These artifacts can be considered scarce from the start, as such long, thin objects were often broken. Thus, a rarity factor must be added to the usual value considerations. Top row: $40.00. (Left to right) Second row: $150.00, $60.00. Third row: $65.00, $35.00, $45.00. Bottom row: $75.00, $50.00, $50.00. (Richard Warren Collection, Missouri)

Blade, Ohio, of blue Coshocton County flint in three hues. This is a mysterious piece, 5¹⁄₁₆" long, having characteristics of three time periods. Concave base suggests early Paleo, basal thinning mainly on one side hints at late Paleo. Beveled edges indicate Archaic. This begins at tip with the usual "right hand" bevel and changes to "left hand" beveling just before midlength. This makes a slight distortion in edge line. All side areas are lightly retouched and no basal grinding is present. This blade is large, very unusual, and in perfect condition. $425.00. (Private collection)

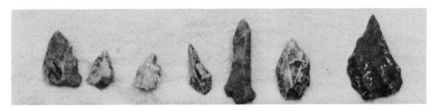

Perforators/awls, southcentral Minnesota, illustrating the highly varied forms of this simple chipped tool. Such artifacts have more study interest than monetary value. (John Kolbe Collection, Minnesota; Carole Revermann, photographer)

Gunflints, probably English and possible trade items; sometimes European gunflints were reworked by Indians. Each $10.00. (John Kolbe Collection, Minnesota; Carole Revermann. photographer)

Celt or ungrooved axe, chopping edge to left, white flint, 3¾" long. Found in Cedar County, Iowa. Age of this specimen is unknown, $13.00. (Christopher Crew Collection, Iowa; Kirk Crew, photographer)

Scrapers, largest 3⁵⁄₁₆", all from Iowa. Top: Side-scraper, white flint, good secondary flaking, $13.00. Bottom row: (left to right) End-scraper, grey and pale white flint, $6.00. End-scraper, white flint with brown specks, $4.00. Edge-scraper, unusual square shape, $5.00. End-scraper, white and blue-grey flint, well-worked tip, $4.00. (Christopher Crew Collection, Iowa; Kirk Crew, photogrpaher)

Drills, various U.S. origins, longest piece 2½" Top row: (left to right) Drill, Michigan, short shaft, $12.00. Drill, Michigan, late-Paleo basal form, fine condition, $100.00. Drill, Arkansas, probably Archaic piece, $40.00. Bottom rows: Obsidian drills, all California, another illustration of the wide diversity of drill types. Note shaft-tip damage/wear, seen on many authentic drills. These are in the $10.00 (left center) to $65.00 (right top) range. (Hershberger Collection, Indiana; Jeff Hershberger, photographer)

Top: Knife, 5¼", quality flint with inclusions, excellent lines, $400.00. Bottom: Base-tang knife, unusually excurvate working edge. This blade is remarkably wide for size, $275.00. (Arnold R. Logan Collection, Texas)

Top: Blade, 6¼", one excurvate and one straight edge, good size and condition, $300.00. Bottom: Blade, 6", nice taper, good lines, $250.00. (Arnold R. Logan Collection, Texas)

Curved scrapers, 4"-7" long, from central Texas and found on all period levels. Values begin at $15.00 and go higher for larger, better examples. (Dwain Rogers Collection; Houston, Texas)

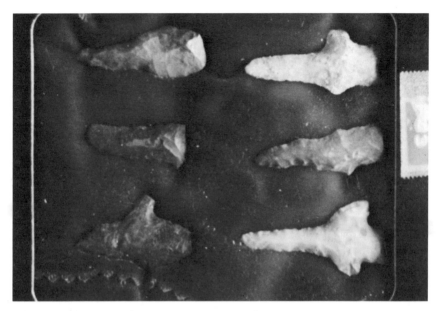

Drills, Tishimingo County, Mississippi, largest piece 3" long. These items sell for $7.00-$20.00 each. Materials are white chert and red jasper. (Dale Richter Collection, Illinois)

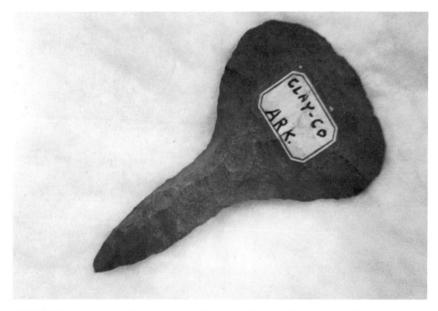

Drill, 2" long, brownish chert, well-round top, with early Arkansas label, $15.00. (Lar Hothem Collection)

Flake knife, high-quality milky translucent flint, 2" long. The 2" beveled edge extends from tip to wide base. There is no evidence of hafting arrangements. While material and fine condition create some value, the irregular form is not a positive factor. This is mainly a study piece, worth several dollars at most. (Private collection)

Paleo artifacts. Left: Rectangular knife, 3¼" long, beveled cutting edge at top, quality mixed flint with orange touches. Right: Flake blade or scraper, edge chipped in from obverse side only, upper left. It is of tan quality Delaware County (Ohio) flint. Such pieces have mainly scientific value and are not usually avidly sought by most collectors. Current values: $100.00 (left); $25.00 (right). (Lar Hothem Collection)

XIII. POINT MATERIALS USED

Collectors know that obsidian artifacts are most common in the West, while flint is frequent in the Eastern U.S. This is generally true, but the story of materials used by Amerinds for points is much more complex.

Actually, there is no official geological material known as "flint." What people call flint is really a crypto-crystalline quartz. It has a structure so fine that often it isn't revealed even under a high-powdered microscope. This material was created eons ago when water, bearing silica, crept into limestone and gradually replaced the limestone substance with silica.

So, flint often contains minute fossils that were in the limestone, but again the tiny objects are now formed of silica. (Silica is a white or colorless compound to begin with and occurs abundantly as sand. Impurities or combinations of them add colors to silica.) In many cases, the fossils resemble tiny rounded grains of rice, or some may be as large as a fingernail.

Chalcedony, or the high-quality flints, was formed in a slightly different manner, but flint and chalcedony are both types of crystalline quartz. For the latter, the material was deposited on walls and hollow spaces, layer by ultra-thin layer, and these gradually built up over the tens of thousands of years. Careful examination can at times disclose the thin layers by a difference in coloration. Some flints were also formed in this way, attested by the very close multi-colored banding.

Flint, chalcedony, jasper, or whatever the regional names, all are primarily the same quartz, colored differently by tiny amounts of impurities. In collector and common terminology, "flint" means medium to high-quality material, while "chert" is used sometimes to denote the lower, duller, grainier varieties. Just where chert ends and flint begins, or vice versa, can be a matter of some debate.

A few flints were formed as nodules, beginning around a tiny fossil or mineral bit, almost as a pearl builds up around a tiny grain of foreign matter. An example is Harrison County flints from Indiana, from which many preform discs or cache-type blades were once made. In fact, prehistoric Amerinds used almost any material that they could chip and that retained an edge or tip reasonably well.

The material so widely known as flint occurs in deposits throughout North America and, unlike some accounts have it, is not restricted to east of the Rockies. No matter the different terms, it is still flint. The material is also found in Alaska, Canada, Mexico and parts of Central America.

Obsidian is also widely dispersed in western North America, usually from the Rocky Mountains to the Pacific. It is a natural volcanic substance much like glass, and it exists in many colors. Obsidian is usually black, brown or grey. A reddish variety is considered very scarce, as are points and blades made from it. Obsidian with green and even blue shades has been reported. This material, in very thin flakes, is translucent.

Interestingly, due to the structural makeup, most obsidian chips better and easier than flint – a fact that must have been known to early chipping artists. Obsidian, like high grades of flint, had considerable value in prehistoric times, and it was widely traded for some distance.

Quarry sources include Obsidian Cliff and several other quarries in what is now Wyoming's Yellowstone National Park. This particular obsidian went into trade routes to make the large ceremonial blades so treasured by the Hopewell Amerinds in Illinois and Ohio.

California's Napa region produced obsidian for area artifacts. Oregon obsidian sources include quarries in Lake County, Deschutes County, and in the Cascade Mountains. Glass Buttes is a famous region with many quarry pits still to be seen. There were other Western quarries, but they are not exactly common. It is remarkable how many obsidian points were made from this fairly limited material resource.

Though the importance of material is briefly covered in the section on value factors (Chapter XV), some brief comments are yet in order. While many points seem to have been purposely chosen for attractive color, this may have been a secondary consideration.

Nice-looking material usually meant a quality flint or obsidian, one that also chipped well and was enduring. That after all was the goal, to make a lasting, useful tool. Fortunately, that long-ago wish produced some excellent points and blades, many in superior materials.

The attraction of good material extends beyond the realm of the dedicated point collector to the general public. For example, flint was chosen as the official gemstone of the state of Ohio. Michael C. Hansen, Geologist, Division of Geological Survey for the Ohio Department of Natural Resources, responds on this status: "Flint was designated as Ohio's official gemstone in 1965 by the 106th General Assembly because this rock occurs in Ohio, particularly at Flint Ridge, in a diverse array of intricately interwoven colors and is highly prized by collectors as a source of material for beautiful jewelry."

Good-grade flint is extremely hard, the very reason points and even broken pieces have existed in virtually unchanged form to the present day. They have survived climatic conditions for uncounted centuries. Again, Michael C. Hansen on the durability of flint: "The resistance to weathering of flint artifacts is not surprising to a geologist as silicon dioxide is very resistant to chemical weathering processes. Indeed, it is an end product of the weathering and erosion cycle ... each cycle removes soft and chemically nonresistant minerals until nothing remains but nearly pure quartz sand."

Hardness has other aspects, both ordinary and almost unbelievable. For an experiment anyone can do, a good grade of flint will actually scratch tempered plate glass. For an experience few would care to share, heart surgery has been performed using obsidian corestruck bladelets. The selection was made because the thin blades had sharper edges than surgical steel scalpels.

On the F. Mohs Scale of mineral hardness, quartz is rated at 7 (on a 1-to-10 basis) and of naturally occurring materials, only topaz, conrundum and diamond are harder. On this particular scale, the quartz family begins the hard minerals.

A listing of U.S. materials and sources for points ends this chapter. Some materials are well known, and a quarry site and brief materials explanation are given. Others are more widely distributed and a general description is provided. Though near-equal mention is made of materials, some, like obsidian, were far more frequently used than, say, gray-wacke.

The listing is by no means complete, but it will serve as an introduction to materials known to have been used by Amerinds for their chipped artifacts. If a quarry or flint-type or obsidian source is known to exist, but further information was not forthcoming – or data was contradictory – the reader is referred to area amateur archeological writings.

One of the fine pleasures and learning experiences for point collectors is to identify the artifact's material and its origin whenever possible.

U.S. Materials Used For Points and Blades

Agate: Fine-grained fibrous chalcedony with bands of color or irregular clouding; found in the West and Northwest.

Agatized coral: High-quality and colorful easily chipped material, found mainly in Florida and parts of the Southeast. It is often translucent and honey-colored.

Alabama flint: Northcentral Alabama, reddish and other hues.

Alibates flint: Texas quarry now a national monument. It has a multicolored flint with a distinctive marbled makeup. Blue-grey is a common combination, as well as blue-banded. There are many other colors, including reds and purples. This was a widely used material ir early times.

Argillite: Point material found in Western Canada, usually black, and can be chipped. It is somewhat of a cross between slate and shale, and is also found in New England areas and elsewhere.

Basalt: Dense, dark volcanic material, often glossy, made up of augite, magnetite and plagioclase; used for points in California and other areas.

Bend and **Burns:** Quarry sites in Oregon; see area am/arc pubs.

Bijou Hills: South Dakota source; see am/arc pubs.

Carter County flint: Kentucky, south of Portsmouth on the Ohio River. This flint is often pastel-shaded and with a curious waxy surface lustre.

Chalcedony: A milky or greyish quartz, often transparent to translucent, with bands of tiny crystals. Some quarries are in the Oklahoma Panhandle region.

Chert: Flint-like materials that are generally not of the highest quality in composition or appearance. Technically, chert is a siliceous rock of chalcedonic or opaline silica, occurring in limestone.

Colorado: Northeastern Colorado source; see area am/arc pubs.

Coshocton County flints and cherts: Ohio, area provided a range of colors in blues, greys and blacks. Widely used in Paleo and Archaic times.

Coxsackie: Eastern New York; see area am/arc pubs.

Dakota quartzite: Found in eastern Oklahoma Panhandle regions; see area am/arc pubs.

Dover flint: Tennessee area, brownish hues.

Edwards Plateau flint: Northwestern Texas, light-colored.

Elkhorn flint: Kentucky; see area am/arc pubs.

Felsite: Northeastern U.S. point material, fine-grained, made up chiefly of feldspar and quartz.

Fishpot chert: Found in the Short Creek area of Ohio and West Virginia. Tan to chocolate brown, it is in nodular form in limestone.

Flint: Very hard fine-grained crypto-crystalline material of the quartz family. It exists in a multitude of grades and colors, is widely dispersed across the country, and was heavily quarried in prehistoric times.

Flint Hill: Source in South Dakota; see area am/arc pubs. Many states have locally known sites with this name.

Flintridge: Multicolored highest quality translucent material. The quarry is near Newark and Zanesville, Ohio. Perhaps the best-known U.S. quarry, the distinctive flint was distributed over much of the eastern part of the country. The site is now a much-visited state park.

Flint Ridge: Kentucky source, near Mammoth Cave National Park; see area am/arc pubs.

Flint Run: Eastern Virginia source; see area am/arc pubs.

Franciscan: Southwestern California; see area am/arc pubs.

Franklin flint: Southwestern Tennessee source; see area am/arc pubs.

Georgetown flint: Texas, a glossy medium-grey color.

Glacial material: Point chipped from a flint or chert that has no known major U.S. quarry site. The material has been transported by glacial activity. It exists either as nodules or rounded sections of "bed" or vein flint.

Glass: Some historic-era Indians chipped points from glass obtained from broken windows and bottles, even telegraph insulators.

Glass Buttes: Famous Oregon obsidian quarry, various colors.

Gray-wacke: A Northeastern dark-grey sandstone containing shale.

Harrodsburg chert: Indiana, a material containing numerous fossils.

Harrison County chert or flint: Indiana, a very widely used substance in early times. It is sometimes known as **Indiana hornstone** and some collectors refer to it additionally as **Dongola flint** or **Golconda chert.** Found in southern Indiana, it is grey to whitish and is in nodular form. Deposits are also in southern Illinois and western Kentucky. This is a well-known regional material.

Hot Springs: Arkansas flint; see area am/arc pubs.

Independence chert: Indiana, and also found in Illinois. It has hues of blue, green and grey and is both banded and clouded.

Indian Creek chert: Southern Indiana; see area am/arc pubs.

Indiana hornstone: See Harrison County chert.

Jasper: An opaque quartz variety, brownish, red or yellow, and rarely in a greenish chalcedony.

Kanawha flint: Found in West Virginia; see area am/arc pubs.

Kay County flint: Northcentral Oklahoma; see area am/arc pubs.

Knife River flint: From North Dakota, Montana and elsewhere, it is brown and tan, translucent, and often with white quartz crystals. There are also other colors.

Lange agate: South Dakota and North Dakota (where it is known as **Knife River** flint), translucent to semi-clear, found between layers of limestone. Colors are clear white, tans through browns, greys, blues and almost-black. (Information courtesy Les Ferguson)

Mill Creek flint: Southcentral Illinois; see area am/arc pubs.

Missouri flint: Central Missouri source; see area am/arc pubs.

Midvale quarry: Idaho; see area am/arc pubs.

Modoc obsidian: Quarry site in Northeastern California.

Monterey: Flint, southwestern California; see area am/arc pubs.

Moss agate: Variety of chalcedony with greenish or other hues.

Niobrira jasper: West central Kansas source; see area am/arc pubs.

Nodular chert or flint: Formed in irregular masses, somewhat rounded and with material indicating concentric rings. In a chipped artifact, these can often be easily seen.

Normanskill flint: New York State, grey to black.

Novaculite: Hard and dense silica-bearing, lighter shades, most are highly translucent. It is found in Missouri and Arkansas with quarries in the latter state.

Obsidian: Natural volcanic glass in many colors, translucent, chipped very well. Even prehistoric chips can inflict cuts on a careless handler.

Onondaga flint or chert: Western New York state, multicolored in blue, grey, black and white. It is often a mottled blue-grey.

Petrified wood: A Southwest and Southern Plains material, this is found in various grades from agate to opal quality, with translucent and glassy characteristics. It chipped with average success and exists in a multitude of subtle colors. A major source was the Petrified Forest area, Arizona.

Pebble or **Gravel Flints and Cherts:** Found throughout much of North America, points were made of this material from flint-like gravel deposits or from stream beds. There is an endless range of quality and color.

Piney Branch: Northeastern Virginia flint; see area am/arc pubs.

Quartz: A common point material for the East Coast regions with ranges from clear ("crystal") to cloudy ("sugar"). Artifacts made of this material are found elsewhere, in the Midwest and Wisconsin. Colors include pink and grey, also amber and blue-green. The state of Washington has a sugar quartz that is brown, tan, pink and yellow. Quartz is silicon dioxide.

Quartzite: A metamorphic material caused by the recrystallization of quartz sandstone, occasionally used for points.

Quitaque (or Quitique) flint: See Tecovas jasper.

Rock crystal: Occasionally used for points; clear, often found in the Southeastern U.S. and in California.

Rock Island chert: Illinois area, blue and grey.

Rhyolite: Fine-grained, igneous, in colors of black, grey and red, often with embedded quartz crystals. On the rough material, lava flow marks may be visible. South Mountain, Pennsylvania was a major quarry.

Sheet chalcedony: Somewhat translucent, in shades of blue and pink. Found in the Bad Lands regions of the two Dakotas and in Nebraska. Sometimes very large blades were made of this material.

Sheet obsidian: Found at least in parts of Arizona in the basic obsidian color range.

Siltstone: A close-grained dull material sometimes used for points in the Northeast.

Slate: Fine-grained metamorphic material, sometimes chipped into points and blades in the Northeast and elsewhere.

Spanish Diggings: Central Wyoming flint; see area am/arc pubs.

Suwanee River: Northern Florida flint source; see area am/arc pubs.

Tecovas jasper or flint: Found in the Texas Panhandle in lenses, boulders and larger outcrops. Colors are similar to **Alibates**, but in red and yellows to blues and greens.

Translucent silicate: A point material used in California and other West Coast areas, especially in early times.

Vitric tuff: Glossy, grainy material composed of compacted and hardened volcanic ash, found in North Carolina.

Wascoite: A brownish material with occasional white portions, from Wasco County, Oregon.

Wichita County flint: Northwestern Texas source, flint obtained from various gravels.

Author's Note: Though some 75 point materials have been mentioned, the number of state and regional flint and chert deposits quarried in prehistoric times is much larger. For example, the states of Indiana and Texas alone each have at least a dozen different material varieties.

Materials differences, all pieces Susquehanna broads, Archaic artifacts averaging 2" long. All pieces are from Warren County, New Jersey. Value range: $5.00-$10.00. (Left to right) Top row: Rhyolite, jasper, quartzite, rhyolite. Bottom row: Jasper, flint, rhyolite, rhyolite. (Bob Lindaw Collection, New Jersey; Joe Hodulik photo)

Material, all Mississippian culture triangular arrowheads, central example 1¼" long. (Left to right) Chert, grey, good lines, well-balanced, $15.00. Fossiliferous flint, displaced fossil at tip (not damage) and fossil embedded at mid-length on right side which creates a rounded bulge, $7.00. Glossy flint, reworked (shortened) point, $6.00. (Private collection)

Materials: Center piece is about 4" long, all from eastern Midwest. (Left to right) Archaic bifurcate, dark flint with "lightning" lines, $14.00. Archaic blade, in rare original form, unsharpened excurvate edges. There is a materials change in the left portion and since flint quality is similar, values are not affected, $200.00. Side-notch, Archaic, uniform glossy black flint, $15.00. (BLH Collection)

Material: High-class glossy white flint, pieces at about 1½". At left, lancehead; at right, arrowhead. Here, design and form are good, but they are overwhelmed by the gem-like quality of fine flint. This adds much to appeal and each point would be valued at about $15.00. (Private collection)

Materials: These three chipped pieces are in excellent condition, have good form, and fair size at 2½". The middle St. Charles is especially appealing, but because of poor material – grainy, low colors, unappealing texture – these examples are worth only $7.00 (left); $25.00 (middle); $3.00 (right). While the authenticity and condition and form/outline are obvious, here the low-grade composition is even more so. (Private collection)

Early Archaic points, illustrating material quality. Left: glossy point, 1" long, black flint with surface sheen, $17.00. Right: drab and dull grey chert in two materials, $12.00. Though of similar type, the large size of one does not mean it is worth more, or the same, as a smaller point of better material. Here, the smaller point is simply more attractive. (Private collection)

Dovetail, translucent Flintridge material. This small "dove" 2¼" long would have been worth at least $150.00 if perfect. Due to tip-side flake removal and badly damaged base at hafting area, the worth is only several dollars. The darker interior material can be seen at both break areas. This is not a Flintridge artifact with patina. Instead, this blade at one time was in a fire. This accounts for surface color and jagged breakage. (Private collection)

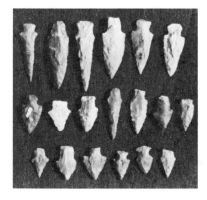

Petrified wood points, 1"-3" in a mixture of tan, red, brown, yellow, orange, white and black materials. These are 2000-1000 BC and are from the Houston Gulf Coast area. The points are colorful, valued in the $9.00-$20.00 range for material content and interest. (Dwain Rogers Collection; Houston, Texas)

Materials, inferior grades. Left: Striated flint triangular piece with concave shaft-smoothing depression ¼" wide at base, tip damage, $2.00. Right: Mottled chert black and grey with white inclusions, 1⅜" long, Woodland-era. Left portion, tip to base, heavily chipped, $4.00. (Private collection)

Material comparisons, left to right: Point, percussion-flaked with base and shoulder-tip material change, actually of little importance in such a low-grade point, $3.00. Blade, reshar-pened, of mottled quartzite. Fair outline, material not particularly desirable, $6.00. Point, in semi-good striated or layered grey flint, 1¼" long. There is also shoulder and base-corner damage, $5.00. (Private collection)

Elora points, Tennessee (left to right): Jasper, 2¾", good gloss, $25.00. Agate, 3", good type size, $20.00. Chert, 2¾", fine edge retouch, $30.00. (Kernaghan Collection, Colorado; Marguerite Kernaghan, photographer)

Rock crystal serrated-edge point, 1⅜", mild damage to tip and base corners, but generally intact. Clear quartz can be considered gem-quality if relatively pure and well-worked, as here, $95.00. (Hershberger Collection, Indiana; Jeff Hershberger, photographer)

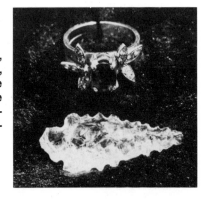

Point materials: (left to right) Stemmed arrowhead, transluscent pink flint, Indiana, $30.00. Obsidian arrowhead, California, serrated, long basal tangs, $45.00. Obsidian point, California, 1⅜", stemmed and barbed, good form, $40.00. Stemmed arrowhead, California, rough material, $7.00. Notched point, Californa, fine form, inferior material, $14.00. (Hershberger Collection, Indiana; Jeff Hershberger, photographer)

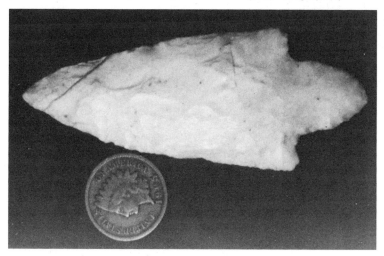

Waubesa, Midwestern point or blade type, Hopewellian (Woodland-era), 3" long. Body is semi-glossy off-white flint, while tip is of chert, a duller grade. The two materials are separated by a thin brown line. An exceptional piece, good lines and balance, $275.00. (Private collection, Florida)

Background: light-colored multi-hued flint with quartz inclusions. Foreground: broken base of large ceremonial flint, mottled blue, with small quartz deposit near top. Quartz can be found in many kinds of flint. (Lar Hothem photo)

Bed or layer flint, large section 6" wide. This was found on an early site, but shows no sign of being worked. Such surface flint is often so weather-fractured as to be useless for points. (Lar Hothem photo)

Nodular flint, mass 5" thick, from prehistoric site. The typical concentric rings can be seen near the top. Most of the outer light-colored layer was chipped off by Indians, leaving the inner portions as source material for artifacts. (Lar Hothem photo)

Unusual flint: (left to right) Early Archaic point, 1¼" long, made of layered or banded flint, $25.00. Bottle-neck Archaic, made of flint with swirls, $30.00. (Private collection)

Historic interest in prehistoric points: This early post-card illustrates a part of Ohio's famous Flintridge quarry with picnic pavilion in background. The fanciful point at lower left was made with "artistic license" and it resembles no known North American Indian point type. (Lar Hothem Collection)

Obsidian: Points and blades from California. (Large points are from northern California; see Chapter VII. Small points are from southern California; see Chapter VIII.) Length range for these multi-hued obsidian pieces is ½"-3"; value range $15.00-$125.00. (Cliff Morris Collection, California; photo by Ray Pace, Associates)

Obsidian: Laurel Leaf and other points, all from Klamath, Oregon. Length is from 1½"-3". (Trade beads and etched bone from same region.) Gem obsidian points and blades of this quality sell from $25.00-$150.00, higher for the larger pieces. (Cliff Morris Collection, California; photo by Ray Pace, Associates)

Plainview, 3", excellent Paleo specimen, in gem material (semi-translucent mottled yellow agate). Tip damage does not detract greatly from good overall lines and material adds to value. It is difficult to find Paleo points without some sort of in-use marks, $400.00. (Gerald R. Riepl Collection, Kansas)

Scallorn, Neo-Indian period, AD 500-1200. Values for good examples: $50.00. Left: Tecovas jasper, Randal County Texas. Center: Alibates flint, Randal County, Texas. Right: Edwards Plateau flint, Crosby County, Texas. (Wayne Parker Collection, Texas)

Rex Rodgers (newly named point), Paleo period 8500-7000 BC, with similarities to San Patrice and Hardaway points. Values for superior specimens go to $140.00. Left to right: Quartz, showing indistinct chipping scars common to the material. River pebble chert, characteristic mottled appearance. Petrified wood, strong, broad base, narrow blade width. Edward Plateau flint, this point very Hardaway-like. (Wayne Parker Collection, Texas)

Fresno, late prehistoric arrowheads, Neo-Indian, AD 800-2000, $18.00 each, all from Crosby County, Texas. Left: Petrified wood, excellent chipping and edge retouch. Center: Alibates flint, good size. Right: River pebble chert, mottled colors. (Wayne Parker Collection, Texas)

XIV. CHIPPING TECHNIQUES

People once thought (and some still do) that Indians chipped flint using heat and water. Supposedly, flint was fired and chips taken off by dripping water on the flint. This rapidly cooled the area, so it was thought, causing material contraction, making a flake fly off. While dramatic and memorable, this theory rides on folklore and discards all evidence.

Points – of whatever style, size or period – were all made in about the same way. Tools of bone and antler were used, and the techniques of percussion and pressure flaking employed. The whole process of point-making consisted of knowing what tool or technique to use, where to strike, the correct angle, and the right amount of force.

Percussion flaking was of two kinds, direct and indirect. For direct percussion, the flint was struck with another object. Entire points have been made with just a hammerstone, though the points were decidedly crude or rough-looking. Percussion chipping usually required an antler or bone mallet or hammer, and large flakes could be removed from any edge. Sometimes a stone anvil was used to brace the flint.

For indirect percussion flaking, reaching areas not directly accessible (like fluting or deep notching) an antler pin or punch was used. The small end was placed at the key spot and the larger end was struck with a stone or club. This allowed great force to be rapidly concentrated on a small area. If the correct impact angle was achieved, a flake of the desired size and thickness was removed.

Pressure flaking was the use of the chipping tool plus the force of hands, wrists and arms. Pressure was applied at the key location until the flake was detached, and surprisingly long flakes can be taken off in this manner. Pressure flaking was used to make shallow notches and to retouch edges, smoothing chipping lines. Often, alternating series of percussion/pressure flaking was done to produce a particular point, as retouch gave a smoother edge which allowed better strikes and more accurate flaking.

The three flaking techniques described made most points and blades, but several specialized chipping techniques were also used. Too, different areas of North America had preferred chipping styles. Paleo edge retouch on some lanceolates, for instance, in the West was usually done with pressure; in the East, with percussion.

But Amerinds were masters of most kinds of chipping imaginable. Fluting was one method, whereby long, shallow flakes were removed from lower face(s) from base toward tip. Several dozen point types had basal thinning done with this bold yet controlled procedure.

Points had the bases prepared for the indirect percussion of fluting in different ways. Some *Clovis* points had a chipping platform ground at an angle, so the punch had a good surface through which to transmit force. Some *Folsom* points had a projecting nipple, used for a similar purpose. It would be a fine thing if one of these points could some day be entirely reconstructed from actual chips to see truly all the stages of point manufacture, from finished point to original chunk of raw material.

Other points received fracture-chipping, which removed edge-slivers of flint, usually along the base bottom, sometimes base/stem sides and lower shouldering. Base fracture areas were usually then ground smooth. The actual fracture-chipping was done with indirect percussion, and some of this work is so well executed in such a small area that it can only be compared to the trained genius of diamond-cutting.

Fracture-chipping was similar to burin-chipping, except the latter drove off only part of a flint splinter. It ended in what is called a hinge-fracture, at about right angles to the force of the blow. Burin-flaking produced a very strong, sharp tip, either at the place of the original strike or at the hinge, or both. The miniature tool that resulted was often made on a flake.

Technology aside, some very beautiful surface effects were achieved by chipping patterns, flake scars, on the point or blade face. Collectors know these marks by certain names and both regularity and precision is sought in such patterns.

Collateral flaking was done equally from both sides of each face, producing balanced sets of chip marks that met at about the face centerline, forming a slight ridge. Transverse flaking was of two kinds. Transverse-horizontal had chipping scars that approached or crossed the face centerline at about right angles and from both directions.

Transverse oblique was angled across the face from about 30 to 50 degrees of arc. There are other, less common patterns. Point styles and types from the Paleo era often have these specialized chipping features.

Bevel edge chipping, or resharpening, was done with percussion flaking, though short bevels on small blades or points could also have been pressure worked. Serrations, or sawtooth edges, were done by spacing the flakes so that small "islands" of flint remained. Usually these teeth project outward in a general sort of way, but a few rare specimens had the serrations pointing backward or forward.

Still another chipping technique was the projection of small, thin knives, struck off from a central "parent" core. A number of early peoples did this and the technique was known from Alaska to Central America.

Midwestern Hopewell Indians specialized in core-knives known as bladelets, and they were often made from very fine flint. A main core was roughed into shape and a striking platform prepared in the area of best-grade material.

A punch was then positioned to strike down the side, at perhaps a 10 degree angle of penetration. Indirect percussion then spalled off the bladelets, and dozens could be removed from a good block. Bladelets were the equivalent of double-edged razor blades, extremely thin, and as sharp-edged as flint was ever worked.

Suggested reading:
Waldorf, D.C. *The Art of Flint Knapping.* Privately published (Box 702, Branson, Missouri 65616), 1975.
Van Buren, G.E. *Arrowheads and Projectile Points.* Arrowhead Publishing Company (Box 1467, Garden Grove, California 92642), 1974.

Left photo: Worked flake, illustrating a fairly rare flint-shaping process, abrasion. Bottom edge of this 2" specimen has standard pressure chipping. However, both other edges have been ground flat, also both faces. Very unusual piece and value is considerable, but only as a demonstration-learning piece. (Private collection)

Right photo: Decatur point or blade, Southeast type, 1½" long, cream flint. It has the diagnostic beveled edge, shallow base, semi-barbed shoulders and fracture-chipping base bottom with one side ground-down, the other still showing the special chipping scar. Age, ca. 4000 BC. Value: $35.00 partly due to rarity. (Private collection)

XV. POINT VALUE FACTORS

Beyond the very basic matter of material used for a point or blade, collectors consider a number of aspects before arriving at a value. Such determinants combine for each point, and will be different for each, if only in the smallest degree. Every point is a singular creation, one more reason why points can be considered prehistoric art.

It is not possible to find two absolutely identical specimens. Nonetheless, certain criteria can be applied when judging the merits of any one point.

Size in important, and large points tend to be worth more than small points. This is because larger pieces usually have a greater visual impact, which encourages admiration which can be converted to a value figure.

There is also the undeniable fact that for purchase comparison, whatever the size, a large point seems to offer more for the money, whatever the amount. This is a surface judgment, however, and often simply is not true. A bigger point is not necessarily better, but size does help and is often the deciding factor as to whether a certain point is obtained for a given amount.

Point thickness, the distance between the two faces through the material, is somewhat of a value consideration, with exceptions. Thinner points, whatever the size, are usually considerably more admired than thick points, in that the point shows more skill in chipping and control over the material. Often such points are better finished as well, so thinness has come to be associated with beauty, of a well-made point.

To be fully understood, the thin-thick aspect must also be two other things, uniform and appropriate. With the exception of tip and edges and often the base, the body thickness should be about the same, with no unsightly protrusions or abruptly shallow regions. Thin-thick must also relate to overall size, and be "about right" for point length and width. This is difficult to explain, but most collectors are well aware of such dimensions.

Some points however, like the Midwestern Fishspear or blades like the Central States St. Charles (Dovetail), were almost always made thick at the center, the latter having a lenticular cross-section. In such examples, the thinness and regularity of the face sides, the edges, still matter. Perhaps the thinness factor can be left with the comment that an otherwise thick point can be well-made in other ways and still retain full collector interest.

Point basal treatment is important, and the more workmanship, the higher the value – so long as that workmanship is of high quality. A plain leaf-shaped or triangular point might be quite good, and some large blades of gem material have sold for very high prices. Generally, though, a point or blade with hafting openings chipped in will command more attention, whether the base is notched or stemmed. The added prehistoric work is thus acknowledged, and the point rightly or wrongly seems somehow more complete. Of course, this does not apply to certain Paleo points that were never notched or stemmed, or to a great variety of knives from all periods, or the late prehistoric triangular unnotched arrowpoints. The overall meaning here is that any extra attention the maker gave the point is of interest to the collector. Finally, some basal work (not all) gives the point a more artistic look.

This is especially true when the signature of the maker is flourished by way of ultra-skilled and specialized work. Two examples are the along-the-face basal fluting done by Paleo craftsmen, and along-the-edge basal chipping accomplished by certain Archaic-era workers. Paleo fluting is thought to have been done to allow shaft-end slimming to give deep penetration into the hunted animals, a means to an end.

An end in itself, edge sliver removal seems to have been a short-cut to dulling, so hafting thongs were not cut through. Both examples are extra touches that add value to the point when well-done and in harmony with the piece. Such deft additions are recognized by the perceptive collector, and are highly valued.

Point workstyle is a strong factor and it is many things. It is how the point relates to the time frame when made, and both how, and how well, a particular artisan fashioned it. Again getting into the art aspect, workstyle might be roughly classed as crude, below-average, average, above-average, superior and superb. Any one point could be judged fairly easily and placed in one of the six classes.

Whatever the material or condition, workstyle predominates, and is a major value factor. What was well-made in prehistoric times is well-regarded today.

The chipping should be regular, showing good control, the ageless proof being in the flake scars that cover all or most of a point. All edges should be consistent, whether straight, rounded or angular, and the whole point should look as if the maker knew what was being done, no mistakes, no afterthoughts. Workstyle on a good point gives one the feeling that chipping techniques had been mastered and that the maker was going about the work with some extra care. (See Chapter XIV for more information on chipping.)

Collectors have great affection for points that are symmetrical – another value factor. While some points and blades were deliberately made off-center (the Southeast Dismal Swamp point, certain Cody knives in the Southwest) or angles in one direction, they are far from common. Symmetry is a sort of perceptual balance, meaning that the left and right sides of a point closely resemble one another, and the best points have sides that are almost mirror images.

Symmetry can be thrown off because the point maker was not preside, or because of damage, or flaws in the material. When symmetry is lost because of damage, a good point is often restored, and visual balance is regained.

Advanced collectors are so concerned about the matter of symmetrics that a point with serrations on one blade edge should have similar serrations on the other. These should be about the same in number, size, location and spacing.

To non-collectors, these would be minute details. To collectors, it is such details that can make the difference between a good and a great point. Further, symmetrics can also apply to an extent to both the front face (obverse) and back (reverse) of a point.

On this, the best of the best points really have two fronts. That is, for displays, the two point faces are so beautifully done and similar and artistic that both sides could be shown to equal advantage. Some old-time (and some present) collectors had points of such perfection and purity that they could proudly be displayed "either side up."

Still, the writer suggests that all points have a slightly better side, and if pushed, the owner might admit to a personal preference, though another collector might disagree. As in appreciating any art form, there are subjective differences of opinion, and beauty is in the eye of the collector.

Even a top-grade point can be marred by material differences or it can be enhanced by them. In average-grade material, the presence of something lower-grade can distract and confuse the viewer, being out-of-place, somehow wrong. But a similar-grade point can also be enhanced by higher-grade material that for some point adds a touch of class.

Material as a value factor has many combinations and meanings. Two or more combinations of about-equal grades but of different colors can co-exist in the point, and – depending on amount, color and configuration – each collector decides whether this is a plus, a minus, or makes no real difference. Foreign inclusions like fossils or quartz crystals are a related matter and can turn up even in the best artifacts. Size and location of such visitors from inner space are keys. At the tip, along body-lines or at the base and showing equal surface on both sides, the presence can be a real attraction.

But, a single fossil or abrupt color change on, say, one shoulder makes an off-center appearance, though the point is otherwise superb.

Each point's circumstance is unique and collectors value such differences in personal ways. Like sunsets, points all have similarities, but no two are ever alike.

Besides the major value considerations already mentioned, there are a number of small things that collectors are aware of, and that many other people might not notice. One is material change or variation from high-gloss to semi-gloss in part of the point. Another might be the fact that one blade side, though apparently the equal in all ways of the other, has slightly more original-use edge dulling.

In very brittle material, sometimes flakes on faces are partly detached or loosened, but do not flake off; there is space beneath them, only a thousandth of an inch thick. These places are always lighter in appearance than surrounding material, since some air is under them, and light reflects differently. It might be noted that some collectors view such curiosities as signs of a recently manufactured point, reasoning that frost action over the centuries would have spalled-off the semi-detached flakes. However, they exist occasionally on absolutely authentic points, and may in fact even have been produced by frost action. But for this discussion, the off-color appearance of several such flakes may have a small bearing on point value. Slight indications of natural spalling is usually accepted, but massive spalling gives an impression of artifact deterioration, which it really is not.

For the average collector, the hafting or notching area of points is of extreme importance. The careful collector also looks to the haft base and – whether it is bifurcated, straight-line, incurvate, excurvate or "other" – requires a baseline of merit. It should be undamaged, well-chipped, consistent with the rest of the point, truly the bottom line.

All these things bring up aesthetics, a fancy word that to collectors means a point's overall impact, its final statement, the large and small aspects of everything. Aesthetics include all of the factors already mentioned, however present in whatever degree. These are psychologically combined in any one point, at least to the collecting mind. In short, how artistic is the point? If it's a rare type, does that rarity add in any way, or make little difference?

Point aesthetics are partly plain to see, and partly never to know completely. It is a vast summing-up that often takes place in a few seconds, and that can even change with time or circumstance or additional information. Collectors can amiably argue the merits and drawbacks of a point for some time, and agree on different conclusions as to how good it really is. The aesthetic aspect is what makes a certain point value acceptable to buyer and seller, and is the bold breath of life to this collecting field. Aesthetics is literally everything.

Beyond well-recognized value considerations – objective charac-teristics of a point and subjective evaluation of them – there are several additional matters of some importance. Though quite different, both can be seen as modern human driving forces, though often not mentioned.

One involves points that to a seller are more than a mere sum of parts. They relate to something memorable or significant. If an unseen meaning is present, the point may have been personally found on a beautiful day. It may have been found under odd circumstances, or may have been the only find on a well-searched site. It remains with psychic strings, something special in the seller's experience, and is priced accordingly.

The point may have been a gift from someone and still retains an aura that it, to the recipient, is no ordinary point. Artifact accumulations that have been in a family for years, even generations, become family heirlooms and may be priced in ranges that go above any known markets.

Another very real aspect is provenance, and the higher values assigned to points with good provenance. The point itself, of course, is not improved, but its value can be. Provenance – the "pedigree" or proof of where a point has been since it was collected – is the historic record of a prehistoric object. While the word is used in a positive way, there can be such a thing as a questionable provenance, even negative, and very many points have no provenance at all. That aside, good provenance on a good point boosts value.

Why should knowledge of who, individual or institution, once had a point matter? In some cases, it doesn't. A minor piece that comes from an unheard-of collection won't produce much monetary excitement. A major point with the sure mark (writing, catalog number, find date and location, etc.) of a respected collector (hence collection, hence individual point) can at times double market values.

Ideal provenance begins with the finding of the point, and these have been picked up in quantities since, on average, the large-scale farming beginnings in the late 1700's. Thereafter – and a point found in 1970 can have an excellent provenance, or a point found yesterday, for that matter – there should be some recorded line of facts as to where the point has been. Collectors usually don't worry too much about provenance except for high-line points and blades, and unbelievably good specimens must have spotless lineage to be accepted as authentic and valuable.

If from an early collection, the chances of a fake origin are decreased because it was acquired at a time when even the best authentic pieces attracted little attention. The old-time collector's reputation for honesty and excellence still attaches to the point, really the key to provenance. Once an acknowledged expert judged it good, worthy of being collected, that goodness remains, perhaps for all time.

While values placed on points, whether in this book or elsewhere, are a valid learning experience, such values are relative. They are true in a general way to the class of chipped art, and specifically to that particular point, at that time, in that location.

It is more important, however, to learn value factors so that they can be applied to any "for sale" point one encounters. Beyond aesthetics are market factors in the area, whether the seller will bargain, and much else. A fair market value can be arrived from different thought avenues, and the more one knows, the easier and more accurate the task will be.

Value factors: Archaic beveled-edge knife, ground notches and base, 3½" long. Light-colored marks on lower face and haft area are glue remnants, not affecting value as they are easily removed. Material is a dull grey chert and shoulder configurations are different – value negatives. Main drawback is the broken base, high in notch area. If of glossy flint, better shouldering and unbroken, this would have been a $150.00-$175.00 piece. As is, $30.00. (Private collection)

XVI. CONDITION

Only about 10%-15% of authentic points and blades are in absolutely pristine, undamaged condition. Most points, then, are not exactly as the long-ago artisan made, used or left the artifacts. Condition has aspects important to points as objects of art and items of monetary value.

Condition means how much of the original point the collector has and the more the better. The word includes material removed by prehistoric use and wear, ancient damage, pick-up and use by later Indians, breaks caused by natural events, historic movement of the land (agriculture, road building) and misuse or accident in the hands of various owners.

It would almost seem that all things conspire to harm these ancient collectibles. They are durable, having existed for thousands of years, but they are also fragile.

There is even a relevant collector term that explains the importance of condition, the word "perfect." This does not mean that the piece is artistically superior or unsurpassed, only that it is undamaged. "Perfect" to the point collector is about the same as "mint" condition to one who collects coins. An undamaged state is always a plus, whatever the other merits of the point. High factors of workstyle and material in a point are all too often nullified by minor damage that collectors consider a major drawback to overall attractiveness.

The most common damage areas are generally the more delicate portions. The tip and shoulder ends are often susceptible to breakage, so also portions of the sides (edges) and base extensions, depending on size and thickness. Due to design, some point types like late-prehistoric arrowheads often have tip damage, while certain beveled edge blades were snapped off at the too narrow hafting portion.

There are certain damage signs one would expect to find on authentic "used" points and such signs are often present. (One day – as farming practices changed to no-till (non-plowing) and fewer points are found to satisfy the growing number of collectors – such damage will help identify non-fake specimens. By then, perhaps, perfect points will be an extreme rarity, and the average collector must fill frames with bits and pieces.) If the prehistoric tool was used, there will generally be signs of such use.

Arrowheads, bow-propelled at fairly high speed, often have impact damage, or if long-stemmed or sharply shouldered, have breakage in those areas. The same is true of *Atl-atl* launched lancepoints, which traveled slower but struck with greater kinetic force, more throw weight. Blades or knives of whatever style or size were used to cut with a sideway or twisting motion, and edge and base damage are common, though tip damage can occur as well.

Similar use damage plagued early Indians and many artifacts show salvage rechipping so the point or blade could still be used. There is growing knowledge that many points considered quite fine by the collector were probably prehistoric throw-aways which had outlived usefulness.

This relates to condition, in that some knowledgeable collectors prefer specimens in as-made instead of as-is size and configuration, wanting new rather than used artifacts. But again, this is a matter of collector taste and interest and should not reflect badly on an undamaged individual piece.

Prehistoric reworking – retipping a point, resharpening a knife – is acceptable if the additional labor does not detract from overall aesthetics and is harmonious with the remaining whole. If the work was done by a much later Indian, sometimes the age-old patina was disturbed, revealing a different color. This, while interesting to study, can also provide a negative distraction in terms of color change.

The two most common damages are chips and outright breakage. Chipping is non-intentional flake removal and can be found anywhere on a point. Rarely, it is even found on the sturdy face, something hard to explain. Most chip-damage leaves the bulk of the point intact and comes anywhere on any edge.

Breakage is another matter, and there is a nearly complete range of seriousness possibilities, from 5% to 95% of a point. That is, a missing tip on an otherwise perfect point can account for the 5%, but if one has that same tip and the rest is absent, there is little to collect. If, conversely, only a small tip is missing, the point retains most bulk and the all-important basal area with key workstyle. Then, a point can usually be easily and accurately restored.

In a collecting field where perfection is the ultimate goal, it is sometimes surprising to non-collectors that, value-wise, a small amount of damage can be very costly. When what would have been a $50.00 point has a base corner missing or shoulder tip gone, this can cut value drastically, and the worth to a collector might be only $10.00. The extreme lower ranges of value come about here because of the frequency of damage and the resultant rarity of non-damaged, highly collectible points.

Discoloration of a point can occur, due to mineral deposits, or exposure of one side only to the elements, be they sunlight or soil leaching. Damage can be permanently etched on points by fire, evidenced by potlid blow-outs (usually on faces), crystalline breakage (often angled across the body) or color changes (anywhere on the point). Often fire damage can be seen on points broken in prehistoric times and such examples with double "hurt" are not very collectible.

Original point damage is usually easy to spot. It will be in use-stress areas, and the break may have slightly dulled edges in some cases, and material interior and exterior patina will be similar. Points broken in later, even historic times will show breakage at unusual places, have sharper edges, and a patina discrepancy.

For badly damaged points, only fragments and bases are valued by some collectors because most of the prehistoric artwork is still present, and the point has lost a relatively small part of its "personality." If one has half a point, it is better that it be the base half.

Any possible tip design has only a few dozen configurations, while bases, due to complexity, have many hundred. In fact, there are people today who purchase broken points, but only the base portions. With these, rechipping is then possible, or restoration with a good chance the built-up parts will closely resemble the original.

The better the condition the higher the appeal and the greater the value. It is unusual for a point to retain monetary worth when much of it is gone. Collectors call these "heart breakers." They are the best part of a fine point, now only a fragment. They retain full artistic merit for what they are, but – like one-third of an early painting or the hand only of a marble Greek statue – they are penalized for what they are not.

Like any art collector, those who accumulate points have different levels of tolerance for damage. What is acceptable to one person might be considered an inferior specimen to another, and the marketplace reflects this attitude. Collectors who might begin by accepting almost anything in the way of Amerind points usually "graduate" to only perfect condition examples, a refection of the desire for wholeness in prehistoric art.

With a chapter of attention given to the importance of condition, it would seem that it is paramount and this is almost always true. However, condition means nothing if the point is fake, and most of them seem to be in the perfect category.

Condition is also nearly meaningless when the point is otherwise mediocre or poor, of secondary workstyle, of third-rate material. Then, condition can be perfect, but the totality is not complemented by the sum of its parts. In such cases, sadly, it doesn't much matter whether the point is in perfect condition or not. No collector is likely to want it or value it in any meaningful way. Fortunately, such examples probably constitute less than 5% of all authentic specimens. Perhaps such points were made by beginners or under emergency conditions, but whatever the source such points are collectible, like fakes, only as examples of what not to collect.

Condition encompasses the whole spectrum, from points damaged into mere fragments to acceptable use or happenstance chip damage to perfect specimens of varied merit. Though each point has a unique beauty, and other things aside, full value goes with the more complete examples. A collector is well-advised to keep this in mind when adding specimens – perfection can't really be improved upon.

Point, 1" long, Eastern U.S., illustrating the reason both faces should be examined. Left: Obverse shows a very average point worth, at most $3.00. Right: The reverse, however, reveals a huge heat-made "pot-lid" that removed about half the original face, making the point just about worthless. (Private collection)

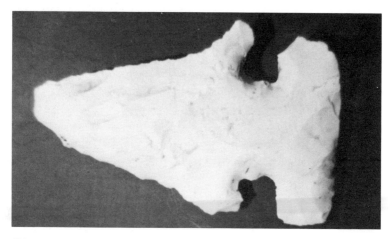

Condition aspects: This E-notch bevel, Archaic era, was reworked until blade edges became irregular (bottom) or incurvate (top). This, plus tip and bottom shoulder damage make the blade an "almost-was" piece. At 3" long, size and good white flint material are a help, condition a hindrance. Perfect, this would have been a $75.00-$150.00 knife; as is, $25.00. (Private collection)

Left: This unlucky Archaic serrated-edge bifurcate, now 1½" long suffered three kinds of damage. Tip was lost in prehistoric times and point was crushed by a bulldozer at a construction site, causing breakage diagonally across the face and the lost section. Perfect, this would have been a $50.00 point. It has no value now to a collector. (Lar Hothem Collection)

Right: Stem and lower sides of very crude blade, 2" long. Little value can be assigned to such a piece with surface deposits which indicate a cave or wet rock-shelter find. Such encrustations on better-grade pieces do affect value, but the extent depends on the individual collector. (Private collection)

Osceola blade, ca. 4000 BC, 3½", brown flint with white stripe. While a superior knife, the missing tip detracts from artistry. Perfect, this would have been a $300.00 piece; as is, $40.00. (Gerald R. Riepl Collection, Kansas)

Condition: Two quite similar Archaic serrated blades, 1½" long, same size, type, etc. Piece at left has good overall outline, $20.00 value. Artifact at right suffers because of reworked left edge that harms aesthetics, $7.00 value. (Private collection)

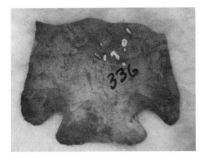

Blade base, 2" long fragment, the type termed "heartbreaker" by collectors when found in similar condition. Of blue quality flint, if perfect, this would be valued at over $200.00. As is, there is only scientific/restoration value. The number refers to permanent ledger record and is a good way to mark points. (Lar Hothem Collection)

Blade, 3⅜" long, mottled blue flint, deeply-notched base. This illustrates the importance of condition. Perfect, this would be a $200.00-$250.00 item. Breakage to left shoulder, left base corner and base-bottom chippage cuts value to $30.00-$40.00. (Private collection)

Late prehistoric artifacts. (Left to right): Arrowhead, Mississippian-era, corner and base-line damage, $3.00. Blade, probably Ft. Ancient culture, bi-pointed light tan flint. Lower right chippage and breakage cuts two-thirds of collector value, $5.00. Arrowhead, Mississippian, with side and basal damage which ruins the outline and collector attention, $3.00. (Private collection)

Condition aspects. Top: Blade, 4" with edge-chips that mar the outline and ruin aesthetics. This slight amount of damage makes a $150.00 blade closer to $30.00. Bottom: Point, pentagonal type. Damage to right base corner and both shoulders, though slight, makes a $35.00 piece worth more like $15.00. (Private collection)

Condition aspects: This Archaic bifurcated blade has been reworked until it became useless. Original length would have been about three times the 1½" of this specimen. A typical collector item in opaque grey flint, there is mild damage to right basal lobe and right shoulder tip, $25.00. (Private collection)

Condition: long blade, 4". Corner-notch (top right) in glossy flint. Perfect, it would be a $50.00 piece. With smaller right barb and damage to right base corner, it is worth closer to $20.00. Stemmed blade (bottom left) light-colored chert. It has stem and blade slightly off-center and has shoulder tip damage, $20.00. (Private collection)

Condition factors: Fragments, averaging 2" long, are eastern Midwest beveled blade midsections with tips and bases missing. Original damage at stress points. If perfect, these would have been $100.00-$175.00 specimens. Now, they are of interest mainly for study purposes. (Lar Hothem Collection)

XVII. FAKES
The Factor of Place And/Or Situation

Knowledgeable sources suggest that there are probably some four or five dozen people in this country good enough at chipping flint to make a living at it. These are the full-time professionals, and there are hundreds of lesser abilities. All turn out points, most of which will sooner or later be up for sale. How many reproduced points and blades are being made? Figuring points from the pros at 1,000 each per year and a somewhat lesser number from all semi-pros, a fair estimate would put the number in the neighborhood of 100,000 points.

Reproduced points, many designed to mislead collectors and cause them to purchase recent copies, are a real problem. As in most collecting fields, there are "forged" examples that cause confusion, anger and monetary loss.

There is a belief around that modern makers cannot chip as well as the prehistoric artisans they mimic, but this is simply not true. Today's chippers can do as well as, or better than, most prehistoric counterparts, though certain age-signs are difficult to produce convincingly.

This said, the place or location where points are available for purchase is very important. Some places are ideal, some are so-so, while others are suspect from the beginning. As always, and wherever, it is still "buyer beware." This means the collector should know something about what is being purchased, *where*, and what this all means.

Auctions are good sources for points, providing some other considerations are noted. Well-established auction firms should be attended, and some specialize in antiques and early Amerind items. With the possibility of reproductions in mind, some have available experts who do not knowingly allow fake points to be sold. While prices (bid wins) may be higher at such top-line establishments, quality and authenticity are usually on hand.

General auctions advertised in classified newspaper sections or handbills can also be good, and the ad usually just mentions "Indian arrowheads." Attending such auctions can be both rewarding and disappointing in terms of authentic points. Sometimes the best points have been otherwise disposed of prior to the sale, often to a semi-interested family relative. Of course, any fake pieces would not have been selected, if known about, and may remain to be sold.

Farm auctions, that old standby of the collector a quarter of a century ago, can still produce good pieces. But today, the farmer is likely to know that "Indian flints" are worth money, and the typical rural seller closely monitors this section of the sale. Too, collectors regularly attend such estate dispersals and it often seems that the more isolated the farm or ranch and the worse the weather, the more collectors and bidders turn up. Sometimes, if someone in the family collected, fake specimens can be mixed in with typical field finds. The fact that points come from a farm does not automatically mean they are good.

Antique shops are another source, but very few dealers know the market value of points or can tell the difference between obviously genuine and blatant fakes. So, the collector goes in armed only with checkbook and knowledge with the second at least as great as the first. Antique shop dealers can't really be blamed as they must keep up with hundreds of classes of items, and Amerind points may command their attention only a few times a year.

Still, the collector may encounter out-of-area points, pieces of uncertain origin – possible bargains, possible fakes. Again, the source cannot be condemned. The burden is on the collector, not the seller, to know the piece and know the price.

Most flea markets do not have a good reputation for authentic points, since in this buyer-seller mart almost anything is offered, at whatever price, and the origin is usually not important. Authentic points are indeed sold and at reasonable prices, but this is not the rule. Too often, fake pieces are in abundance – large, "showy," and low priced. A lot of money has gone for bad pieces at such places and some collectors avoid them as a matter of principle.

Flea markets are a hectic world, an experience of seeing many things in a short period of time. The harried carnival atmosphere is conducive to spending money. Country fair, pawnshop, and bargain day rolled into one, collectors must be careful not to become caught up in the "buy it" syndrome. Just as there can be auction fever over mediocre pieces, so is there a flea market state-in-mind that can sometimes lead to a bad purchase.

Mail-order can be a problem in that there is usually no opportunity to examine the points before purchase, and one must rely on the dealer's description or photos. Reputation of the seller is all-important and there are indeed good mail-order people who provide authentic points at reasonable prices. One must be extremely careful, however, when rare examples are being offered at prices a fraction of what such works usually bring.

Beyond the factor of fakes in terms of place – which really involves common sense above all – there is the matter of circumstance. Whatever the setting – flea market, shop, yard sale – it is assumed that the points can be viewed or even handled at some leisure. This means the points can be studied and compared to others, a very worthwhile thing.

Are there too many point similarities? For example, are the points less than skillfully chipped from larger flakes, which generally leaves one face smooth? While an occasional late prehistoric arrowhead or earlier point was made in this manner, it would be abnormal to find dozens made in this "shortcut" fashion. This is a common method of faking points, done by semi-skilled workers with access to a supply of large flint flakes. The points are never expensive, often 1" or 2" long, with large notches. The points generally look like a caricature of what the maker thought an arrowhead should be and may be offered at about a dollar each. Actual material may vary, but the style does not on these low-level fakes.

In any flint grouping, one should very much beware of points or blades chipped from the same material, no matter whether the grade is high or low. The average authentic assemblage will have points made of materials from any (or at least several) different sources, depending on which prehistoric peoples went where for good quarry material.

Since certain quarries were often in favor with different Amerinds, one source material is unlikely. Also, authentic finds are likely to be of different materials due to the manner in which points are typically found.

The only possible explanation for a number of authentic same material points done in similar workstyle is a *cache* find. These are underground deposits of points, buried long ago for whatever reasons. But such finds are very rare, often make at least local news when found, and tend to end up in hands of advanced collectors. It is almost unheard of (unless of poor quality) for such objects to be offered at low prices for the finder very quickly becomes aware of the treasure-trove value aspect.

When points are available, no matter how mixed the material, of only a certain type, this may be a sign that the recent maker achieved mastery in one direction. Often such examples are of a much-admired point or blade type, but there is little variation on the single theme. There is a certain sameness that would not ordinarily occur, and the buyer would do well to avoid such offerings.

Also, points that are similar in most ways (for example, size or material) but have bases that are different are still not always authentic. This just means that the maker knew how to throw in some confusing differences, copying the random styles one would expect to find in a genuine grouping.

Another level up in the world of fakes is the collection that has a good range of sizes, divergent materials, and a scattering of point and period styles. At first glance, this sophisticated arrangement offers good points at market prices, but there is yet the circumstance of workstyle.

There is a semi-famous "truism" that states "Once is accident, twice is coincidence, and three times is a pattern." This should be considered in viewing such a supposedly good grouping – this in terms of workstyle. Are the points about the same thickness? Are percussion-flake scars about the same size and depth on the two faces? Is the pressure-retouch (if present) of the same regularity? Do all edges have a similar degree of sharpness or dullness? If so, these are signs to exercise extreme care.

Often when points are offered, the seller has other Amerind artifacts. If the stone axes all look alike and the pottery was made in Hong Kong, there's no reason to believe the chipped artifacts are much better. The source, in short, must be as good as the items offered.

Most collectors also tend to wonder about any collection that has all points in absolutely undamaged condition. Unless the points come from a collection known for perfection, the question must remain. Points tended to be damaged down through time, or at least have certain age signs. So if perfection predominates and at suspiciously low prices, the buyer can all too easily acquire bad pieces.

The collector learns rather quickly to keep away from such everyday fake offerings in terms of "circumstantial evidence." The most difficult of all situations, even for a long-term expert collector, is this: There is a grouping of obviously authentic points offered and the seller is likely to explain that they were purchased from a retired farmer, or give some other story the collector wants to hear. "They've been in the family for years" will do nicely. The story may even be true. But, mixed with the average-quality points are several super points which were never chipped by a prehistoric Amerind. Such fakes, knowingly or unknowingly acquired by the seller, can be a problem, especially if very well done.

The circumstances are good, the desired point being part of other old pieces, but fake pieces must still be identified as fake pieces. The collector's strong desire, or wishful thinking, that the point is good does not change a thing.

Some collectors get around the whole problem by dealing only with other collectors, buying, selling, trading. Collectors, due to a deeply shared interest, tend to trust one another until the approach seems unwise. All have similar expectations and fears and even beyond the collecting, good friendships can result. Only rarely is the trust misplaced and word quickly gets around.

Some collectors decide to go to the source. They purchase point accumulations directly from the finders, either surface hunters or farmers and ranchers. At first glance, this is good, for the farmer gets cash for accidental cultural litter gathered while making a living in another way. The collector gets in, literally, on the ground floor and buys points ahead of the competition.

However, individuals have been known to trade spectacular fakes to the finders for authentic points. The result is that what would normally be a suspicion-free group of points now has a scattering of bad goods. In addition to cheating the finders, such fake pieces cast doubt on the whole point collection, further confusing matters.

Before assuming a field found collection is all good, the collector should determine whether any points have been "traded in" or if there are also purchased points. Not all trades are necessarily fakes of course, but a buyer should still know about them.

One of the better ways to acquire fake-free points is to buy an old collection that has passed down through several generations and has not been added to in recent years. If the provenance of the group as a whole is satisfactory, it is likely that all points are authentic.

For many years, it has been a saying among collectors that field-found points had to be good, and for many years, this was true. That is, if the artifacts were picked up on a prehistoric site, there was no chance fakes were present. Now, however, there are scattered reports (rarely documented) of fake points being "seeded" onto sites, to be found by friends or rival collectors.

In the first instance, such work has been done in the way of practical jokes. The person who put down the piece even sometimes steers the unsuspecting finder-to-be in the correct direction during a surface hunt. To further the humor, in one case the chipped blade had been marked "Genuine Indian Made."

In the second instance, there is a more serious effort to introduce bad points into someone's collection. If in fact this occurs with any regularity anywhere, there are several explanations or possibilities. One collector might want to see how well another could identify fakes, or it could be an effort to downgrade a collection or reputation. More likely, one person is attempting to "decoy" people away from a favorite hunting site, to have them spend time in an otherwise unproductive area.

Place, circumstances, situation – all are important determinants of whether a point is good, questionable or fake. If there is any problem at all as to whether points are authentic, it's best to pass them by. One does not always need to learn the hard way, and there are plenty of good points available at reasonable prices. Here, doubt can be a blessing, and suspicion a very healthy attitude.

Reproduction blades, photographed at a flea market. The similarities of size, flatness, chipping patterns, edge treatment, material and perfection are signposts of modern-made artifacts (Lar Hothem photo)

XVIII. FAKES – The Point Factor

A story makes the rounds – Before a major Indian artifacts show, a resident of a nearby hotel is kept awake into the morning hours. The reason isn't a boisterous party in the next room, but the brittle clicks of someone chipping flint.

Perhaps apocryphal, the tale still illustrates one fact. While you read this, someone is turning out a pretty fair copy of points you like to collect. Many of these points are so well done that even some experts won't call them good or bad for certain, only "questionable."

Few modern flint-knappers achieve such levels of skillful deception, but the points exist and in increasing numbers. The collector has some strong defenses on his or her side, and the greatest of these is knowledge. This begins with an awareness of point types being faked.

The best efforts are not being concentrated on below-average points worth only a few dollars, but on pieces normally valued at $20.00-$25.00 and up. Top line fakes in the $100.00 and up category are all too prevalent and many $300.00 pieces were "born" a year or two ago.

It should be stated that there doesn't seem to be any one fail-safe method for determining fakes, since the points are so different, the techniques varied. A whole group of considerations is helpful, beginning with the appearance of the point. Is the chipping too fresh, too recent-looking?

Except for late historic arrowheads several hundred years old, projectile points will average in age well over a thousand years and some are many score centuries old. Weathering on most types of material changes the surface color or texture so most points will look fairly old.

Edges should not be too sharp for this is another indication the point did not rest in the ground for a long period, where it would have been subjected to erosion forces and temperature differences. Test this by first examining the edges of similar authentic points. Then, lightly feel all edges. Touch can be almost a subconscious sense and with time good points will "feel right." Some blind persons can in fact feel differences as small as 1/10,000th an inch.

Points also should not be made of the wrong material for period, in the wrong style, or be too large or too small for the type. All this can be learned by studying literature and by talking with those collectors who are also concerned about fakes.

Sometimes, if a point is questionable, it is even possible to locate a piece of the same material, and chip it yourself to see if the surface characteristics for recent work are similar. If so, and the material normally weathers heavily, the point is probably no good.

Much is made by collectors about *patina,* what material has it, what it means. Patina can be any number of things, including how the word is pronounced (*pat*-in-uh) and it means a thin coating on the material surface, a layering. It can be color changes, texture differences, or chemical additions from soil or water.

To confuse matters even more, some authentic points – which apparently had one side or face exposed to sun or earth – have very different patinas on the two faces. This in itself is probably a decent sign of authenticity.

Fakers can artificially patinate points to a certain degree, and one method is to place the point in "hard" water and boil the brew done. Several chemicals will adhere to the point, giving a certain antique appearance. Unless further treated, the point will have an abrasive feel.

Another method is to place a new point in a rock tumbler for 45 minutes with grinding material to dull fresh chipping marks and give an aged appearance. This wear will be overall, which means it is too light in some areas for real wear, too heavy in others.

The writer personally admires points with old ink inscriptions, these usually giving a place, date and perhaps the finder's name or initials. Related are the sometimes unreadable catalog marks of long-forgotten collectors, whose connecting records have become lost with time. Too much should not really be made of these finder-collector markings (sometimes in handsome early script) as some fakers are now adding false historic inscriptions on better points.

The point factor means that individual points separated from helpful context must be closely examined. Wear signs can be faked but are still to be watched for. Few Amerind points are exactly as the artisan made them but were reduced through use wear. Some we collect were really worn out and tossed away, of no further utility then, but top pieces today.

If a knife, the edges may show considerable rechipping and many examples have the two edges showing very different chipping, wear, or use damage. If a point, there may be tip or base signs of use.

Scrapers (not normally faked, as collector value is low) should have edge-polish, which can be seen by glancing along the curve. Sometimes faint use signs can more easily be felt. Chipped drills of average length might have some shaft polish, but this is not the case if the "drills" are worn-out knives or extra-long hairpins.

Scientists sometimes study chipped artifact edges with micro-scopes and compare the tiny marks with tools used for specific purposes. Deer-skinning, clam-opening, bone-cutting – all procedures left distinctive imprints. The collector, on suspicious pieces, would do well to learn about such evidence.

Signs should include not only how a point was used but how it was made. Chipping patterns should be correct and any base-dulling should be noted. Countless examples show basal grinding and this was typically done in certain ways and styles.

Sometimes the main problem isn't how the artifact was chipped, but *what* was made. Certain categories seem to have more than their fair share of spurious objects, and these include "thunderbirds" and other bird or animal effigies, fish hooks, and long pins or drills. If any chipped object is not known to belong to an authentic class, they are best ignored as being somewhat, or totally, suspicious.

Some collectors swear by ultraviolet lamps or "black light" devices, saying fakes can be spotted by color variations. Having seen demonstrations, but with few conclusive results, the writer is frankly uncertain of the value of these devices for point collectors. It would seem, however, that in special cases ultraviolet might be useful, as in determining reworked or restored areas of an authentic point. The key would be not so much what the light revealed, but in understanding what such revelations mean.

While not exactly fakes, authentic Indian-made points can honestly be only a few hours old. Some Amerinds – such as the North Carolina Cherokees – chip points for sale to tourists. A similar situation exists in the Southwest, involving inexpensive "Apache" points.

These points, though rather unsophisticated, are usually purchased by a casual family member, not a collector, unless an example point is desired. These are the points commonly seen in gift shops and at "Indian village" shops. To the writer's knowledge, such points are not marked as being of recent origin.

Collectors most value whole or perfect points, and sometimes a good point is field found in several pieces. Or, a complete point is dropped and broken during collector handling, show-and-tell in a school classroom, or by "playing Indian." Such broken points are sometimes put back together with modern glue and offered as complete.

Individual specimens should be examined for three tell-tale features. With little additional explanation required, these are surface-visible "hairline" cracks, dried-glue beading or seepage anywhere along the fault join, and minor edge chip marks along the crack. Break areas may be mid-length, but special attention should be directed at the more vulnerable tip and base areas.

Point "improving," unfortunately, is an occasional practice among collectors and it has many forms. Whether done quickly just after a point is field-found or more carefully at home, the procedure is done to make the artifact more pleasing or attractive, hence, collectible. Some collectors who hate fakes still see nothing wrong with a few brief chips here and there, adjusting condition and aesthetics from what-is to what-it-ought-to-have-been.

Examples seen: One blade shoulder is too low, so it is chipped back to resemble the other. One side has serrations that go beyond those of the other side, so several are knocked off for balance. Or the tip isn't quite sharp or centered enough, so it is re-balanced into the rest of piece. Such hopeful, and fresh, chipping should be apparent, providing the buyer looks for it and recognizes it when seen. This has been done on points in all value ranges.

Advanced "improving" of authentic points, faking on a partial scale, has been done since the late 1800's. Usually, a semi-skilled flaker will rework a valuable point or blade, providing a new tip, edge or base. Some crypto-crystalline materials simply do not develop, or at least show, a patina and recent chipping will go unnoticed. Very light and very dark-colored materials seem to hide modern reworking rather well, but this is not always true. At times, in a triangular or leaf-shaped blade, notches or stemming are chipped in and without obvious changes.

This sort of advanced improvement not only cheats the prospective collector but is unreal to the original form, making it a partly untrue art object. No matter how minor the alteration, such changes tend to further confuse point typology. The collector is again advised to study authentic points and learn to recognize chipping that does not belong to that type or is wrong for the piece.

Point restoration, getting it together, is a perfectly honest way to try to complete a point. Restoration adds what is missing, and the final product thus looks somewhat like the original artifact. Usually a pliable substance is moulded into position, allowed to harden, and then has chip marks carved in with a razor. The section is then colored to resemble the original material.

Certain point or blade areas are typically restored. These are the complete tip, side sections, and shoulder or tang parts, plus stem or base area. With base intact, and sides present, it is easy to visualize the tip. With only the tip and some sides, it is impossible to accurately render the original base-area design.

A restored point, depending on the individual collector, is aesthetically valued somewhere between a broken artifact and a complete point. But always, the less restoration the better, unless the restoration appears better done than the original point, in which case it was probably not worth being restored.

Many collectors restore points, and their efforts are perfectly acceptable for display purposes. A few persons do professional caliber work and sometimes the additions or repairs are quite difficult to detect. A problem develops when restored points (though never usually completed to deceive people) enter the marketplace unmarked, as complete specimens. So there is a chance that a previously owned point might have restored parts.

There are ways to detect such points, however, and the point should be examined in the most likely areas of restoration. The color can never be an exact match under good light and close scrutiny, and neither can be chip mark scars duplicate the flaking of the original maker.

Surface texture, seen against slanted light, should also provide the signs of juxtaposition flint and composition. Touch can also follow up any suspicious signals, as texture changes not only look but feel different.

The quickest and surest test is should. Take another thin piece of flint and rub or lightly tap on its edges and also on suspicious parts. There will be a rapid sound change from ultra-hard to relatively soft material, and this proof is conclusive. The sound will usually go from a higher to lower pitch.

While not really fakes, some people attempt to add the gloss that denotes high-quality material by spraying points with clear lacquer or varnish. This can usually be detected by uniform light reflection and an obvious thin surface coating and/or bubbles can be seen. Authentic and fake points have both been treated in this fashion.

There is an area that should be mentioned, though it is one not likely to cause trouble when a point is closely examined and held. This is the modern class of totally created or cast objects. They are used for display purposes, scientific stand-ins, or as teaching aids. Such works were often made from moulds surrounding actual and authentic specimens, so at least the general form is correct.

Material range is wide, from various metals to plastics. Tip-offs are color, often a single dark blue hue in the military-grey range and weight, which is either too heavy or too light compared to flint or obsidian. Today, color-tinting is sometimes used, and the specimens are amazingly similar to the real object. When a collection is obtained, each point should be closely examined so that no cast points are included.

Point-faking has been around for over a century, and skill has increased in that time. Any desired point type can be made and be well made. Collectors feel that fakes usually come from some area of the country other than their own, being suspicious of "outside stuff." The fact is that fake points are everywhere and no area of the country is fake-free.

The matter of fake chipped objects is so important, in the writer's opinion, that this largest book chapter is devoted to the subject. It is further expanded by the following section, excerpted from the publication "Detection of Fraudulent American Indian Artifacts," sub-section "Chipped flint." It was written by A.J. Wesolowski and is reprinted here by special permission.

The publication is available from Mr. Wesolowski at 7125 E. Fanfol Drive, Paradise Valley, Arizona 85253. He is proprietor of the well-known World-Wide Artifacts, Inc.

"Beware of all flint turtles, buffaloes, lizards, thunderbirds, fish hooks, and generally all eccentric shapes made of chipped flint. There are a few authentic weird shapes, but they are very rare. For example, there were only two eccentric points out of a collection of 10,000 projectile points, and these two did not represent anything in particular. Can you imagine a flint fish hook catching a fish?

"Many newly made arrowheads are now on the market. These can be detected quite easily because of no patina on the flint. Many arrowheads are rechipped, that is points are made of broken pieces or notched from triangular ones. Generally the newly chipped portion will have a different color or tone than the rest of the point and can easily be identified. Some flint, especially Flint Ridge material, doesn't weather and rechipping is hard to detect. However, even in this case, newly chipped flint will have a sharper edge or will have little spalls adhering to the main body of the point. These can be brushed off with difficultly – nature does this in time as elements such as water, frost, temperature change, etc. will loosen these little spalls.

"Obsidian is a very easily worked material and so, naturally, many frauds are made of this volcanic glass. However, a scientist can tell the age of an obsidian surface by a simple microscopic examination. An expert on obsidian artifacts can detect a freshly chipped piece just by observation.

"Some projectile points are aged artificially by spraying lightly with colored lacquer. Lacquer thinner applied to the piece will remove this artificial patina. Then some flint is etched in hydrofluoric acid, but this leaves a distinct whitish coast to the surface, much like etched glass. Other points are covered with organic material such as oil or syrup, and then baked at a high temperature, say about 500 degrees F. This a very difficult to detect as the organic material carbonize and even runs into the surface crack, making it almost impossible to remove. However, these points look unattractive, so the price is low anyway.

"All stone, especially flint, obsidian, or basalt has a "grain." (This is a controversial point, but I found it to be the case in my experiences.) This is the principle behind the Neolithic core industry. The flint knapper finds this grain and prepares a core of the material in such a manner that he can strike off long sharp flakes, appropriately called core flakes. These then are fashioned into projectile points and other tools. Modern man has found a technique to make these long beautiful flint spears. The process consists of finding the grain of the flint, then sawing the flint into thin slabs parallel to the grain. Then the slabs are pressure chipped or flaked in a drill press, where a pressure can be transmitted to the edge of the flint slab, producing a fine symmetrically chipped artifact. So beware of large ceremonial spears over 6" long. Watch for flatness of the spear; the real thing will most likely have a very distinct curvature and will not be parallel. There may also be saw marks on small flat places, as the faker often misses little spots. Also watch for newness of the surface, and don't forget the low price. A fine genuine flint spear 10" long can easily be worth over $1,000.00! Corner-tanged knives or spears are quite rare. It is estimated that 95% of them floating around are fakes.

Most all fine looking Paleo points on today's market are also fraudulent. More than one enterprising white Indian has rediscovered the secret of fluting a spear in the manner of the ancient big game hunters. Be very wary of all Paleo projectile points including Folsom, Clovis, Scottsbluff, Yuma, Cumberland, Dalton, Quad, Eden, etc. On these types it is almost better to have some slight damage, so the surface patina can be seen by contrast. There are even smaller dovetails and beveled spears being made of grey or brown Indiana and Kentucky flint, so look these types over very careful and consult an expert, as these can command quite a high price." – AJW

No collector should quit the field, as some have, thinking that everything is fake. This is not the case at all, though one should still be aware that certain point types are copied with greater frequency than others. The ever-learning collector will increasingly be able to tell what is good and what is bad, plus what is suitable for the collection. This is simply a case of knowing that fakes exist, and that the problem is serious. Here, forewarned becomes forearmed.

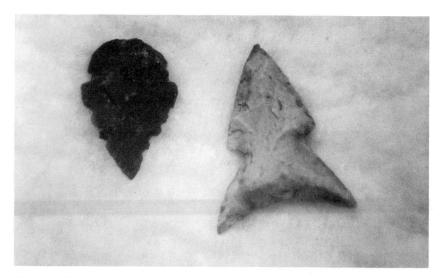

Fakes (left to right): Point, of the casual, unskilled type turned out by the thousands in and near the Southwest. Points, all edges the same degree of sharpness, questionable point styling, base too thick. This may have been made from an original blade tip, one method of modern manufacture. Value: none. (Private collection)

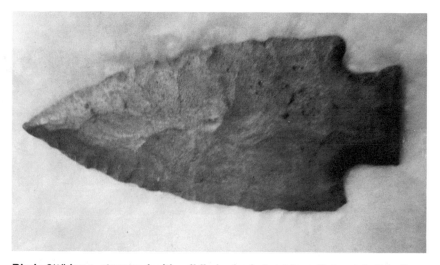

Blade 3⅛" long, stemmed with mildly barbed shoulders. Extremely thin (less than ¼"), this is a very well-chipped piece in a quality brown flint. Very balanced blade body. Made in a basic style and thinness and size as employed by many fakers, this is yet an authentic find from a prehistoric site, $60.00. (Private collection)

Fake points and blades. The growing sophistication of the modern pointmaker is well illustrated in this photograph. Once, every fake point was perfect, without apparently "honest" damage. Today, minor damage is being put into the points. This damage is listed here for each point. (Left to right): Missing left stem corner; irregular edge, mismatched shouldering; right shoulder tip missing; shoulder higher than mate. Value: Instructional only. (Logan Collection, Texas)

Fake points and blades. Top: Pedernales copy, implausibly long since the average length is 3"-3½". Left: Folsomoid copy, probably an effort to make a Plainview, with slight damage to right side and tip, the final touch. Right: Calf Creek copy, with stem that should have expanded slightly toward base instead of tapering. Also, the usual basal-thinning scars are absent. (Logan Collection, Texas)

Fake Folsom point, 2¼" long. This is a beautiful piece, with excellent shape and fluting on both faces. Suspicious signs: colorful material of type not generally used, all edges same amount of sharpness, edge contour not quite right in that shouldering is usually higher and of more abrupt angle to tip. Value: none. (Private collection)

Fakes or modern reproductions unmarked as to true origin. Left to right: Drill, 2" long, perfectly balanced specimen but with all edges sharp and the same degree of sharpness. Fish hook, thoughtfully notched to show where "Indians" would have fastened the line. Same edge treatment as companion piece. Instructive value to collectors only. (Private collection)

Authentic improved specimens, two of three. Left: Old authentic blade but with modern chipped notches in an attempt to increase attractiveness and value. Center: The same as left example. Right: Fake point, rather rough notching. On many authentic corner-tanged blades, if a line is drawn from notch center angle to blade edge, that intersection is between ¼ to ⅓ the distance down blade, base corner to tip. Example on left missed entirely; on center piece, tang was angled about right but few corner tangs were otherwise so crudely finished. (Logan Collection, Texas)

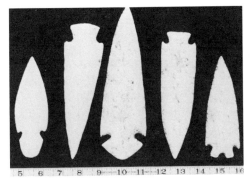

Reproduction blades, showing great size and the usual fine condition, undamaged outline. Instructional value only. (Hershberger Collection, Indiana; Jeff Hershberger, photographer)

Fake drill, often available at between $35.00 and $75.00 for this 7" specimen, made up to look like a fantastic ceremonial item. If authentic (and few Amerind drills are this long) it would be worth in excess of a thousand dollars. All edges are sharp, size too great, unknown origin. Value: none. (Private collection)

Fake blade, Eden or variant type, 5" long. All edges have been ground on this fine-looking reproduction and it is a bit thick for type. Super pieces in fabulous condition should always be suspect, if the true origin is unknown. Value: none. (Private collection)

Reproduction point 2⁹/₁₆" of high grade cream-colored chert containing tan streaks. This point is very thin and flat, quite well made, the work of an expert contemporary flint knapper. It was purchased for $10.00, ca. 1978. If old and Indian-made, the value would be four to five times as much today. (Private collection)

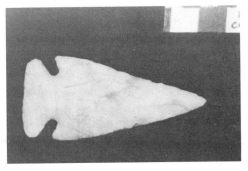

XIX. ACQUISITION GUIDELINES

If there are any great truths about collecting Amerind points, they are these: collect what you know, what you can afford, and always, collect carefully.

The first goes beyond obtaining what one likes. What one can live with is fine for antiques as home decor, but points are a bit different. Acquiring what is truly known about, in terms of type and overall quality, has several positive aspects. The points are likely to be good examples that add both to collector knowledge and collection value and the problems of fakes is almost eliminated.

Collecting what is familiar is not the same as obtaining carbon copies, for point differences are endless. It does mean that in an increasingly complex world of available points, the collector acts with the welcome sureness born of good knowledge. One chooses from among competing points by knowing, not so much what looks good, but what *is* good.

The second, the money matter, is a highly personal thing and Americans tend to be more close-mouthed about financial affairs than the other kind. But the question remains: how much should be put into an arrowhead collection? There are several answers to this, like "as little as possible" (buy low) or "as much as possible" (there won't be many top-grade pieces like these again). It is a private decision, weighed against other realities.

Point collecting is a matter of deciding how much of that famous "discretionary income" – what's left over after the bills are paid – can or should go for good points.

Some serious collectors budget and set aside a monthly amount and do not go over it. Others, with a cash windfall, finally purchase a long sought-after collection and negotiations for such deals can last for years. Still others take cash to auctions and stay while the money lasts.

In an almost mystical manner, collectors seem to manage acquisition of what they really want. The last word on this sometimes seems to be that the mortgage gets paid, points come next, and food and transportation needs get met – maybe.

The third acquisition guideline, buying carefully, means making the best decision based on all available information. No person can have complete expertise in all areas, and careful collectors do not hesitate to ask for advice from others more knowledgeable. The collector must also be willing to discard such information if it conflicts with what is solid fact. The collector must become an independent thinker, for decision sharing or shaping can only be spread so far. Each point acquisition situation is a bit different, whether the purchase is a point worth $2.00, $200.00, or $2,000.00.

Some collectors specialize in trading, either point-for-point or points for other collectibles. This is a world unto itself, and some points tagged at high prices can be traded for others with similar markups, though such values would never be bid at auction. The collector to succeed at this must not only know Indian points, but also possess some bartering skill.

There is an ageless question: Why is a $75.00 point worth three $25.00 points? Is it really? If there are satisfactory answers, a trade can be to the benefit of both parties, with the wanted exchanged for the less-wanted.

A good Indian point collection should eventually have some focus, so long as the emphasis has meaning to the collector. This may mean points of a few top materials, or types, or points from a certain period or area or site. Then the assemblage becomes something more than frames of individual points, having more meaning and information value.

Few people anymore can, or care to, collect everything in Indian chipped art, the "shotgun" approach. This is due partly to increased competition and higher prices, also to the fact that intermediate and advanced collectors tend to specialize. This "rifle" approach is one way to achieve a best-of-class collection.

The ultimate point collection, by the way, would contain one fine specimen of each of the 500-plus type points (already named and to be discovered) in North America. Such a collection could theoretically be assembled, but new names are added each year. So the collection could only be begun, never completed.

Beyond the collecting area or focus, most good collections also have a certain "thrust" or direction. This not only satisfies the collecting drive or impulse, but has value for the future. Such direction might be constant upgrading, enlarging, or authenticating. Points might be obtained with an eye on what other collectors want, at least at this time, adding to overall value.

In all probability, in the long-term view, what collectors want now is what collectors will always want – good points, fine condition, and fair prices.

While the problem of fake points will never go away, one must say they certainly add to the challenge of collecting original and good points. They at least have recognized that old points are an art form and have spent years trying to duplicate that art. They have become experts in their work which is rarely seen in action, only in result.

Self-education in the field is very important. Nowhere is a college-level course being offered on how to acquire a good point grouping and very little has actually been written about it. Because of the complexity of Amerind points, this is one of the more difficult collecting fields today – difficult, that is, in terms of collecting well.

Collectors should, as soon as practical, start a library of good books relating to point collecting and several books were suggested earlier that encompass regional point types. The writer also recommends membership in organizations that not everyone knows about, the amateur archeological societies. They are made up of collectors and students interested in knowing what chipped points and other Amerind works they have and how the artifacts fit into the prehistoric lifeway. State or regional in membership, regular meetings are held that offer much information on points, good and bad. The societies are strong proponents for preserving as much of the chipped art past a as possible. Some societies have fraudulent artifact committees made up of persons skilled in detecting fakes and authenticating good points.

The collector is strongly advised to join one or more such organizations, especially those that cover his or her geographic area. Contact with other nearby collectors is beneficial and most am/arc groups put out quarterly journals that are both readable and accurate.

These publications serve as fine research sources for that unusual point that no one has been able to identify. (In fact, over 250 issues from various societies were studied in preparing to do this book.) A listing of am/arc groups concludes this chapter and includes the society's official publication.

The field of point collecting is fascinating, even hypnotic. That's good, in that interest in points can be an ever-growing thing with many bold and subtle satisfactions. But it can also be taken too seriously. Upon occasion, a person becomes totally engrossed, spending a great deal of time and money. In the rush of discovery, obligations like employment and personal relationships have been downplayed with unforeseen results.

As in most things, one beauty of point collecting is to reach a certain balance with the rest of life. The goal is not to overwhelm that central core of existence but to enrich it.

Amateur Archeological Organizations

You may write directly for membership or other information.

Organization	Publication
The Archeological Society of Virginia 562 Rossmore Road Richmond, VA 23225	*The Quarterly Journal*
The Piedmont Archeological Society 2121 Quail Drive Harrisburg, NC 28075	*The Piedmont*
The Archeological Society of Ohio 2505 Logan - Thornville Rd. Rushville, OH 43150	*Ohio Archaeologist*
Central States Archeological Societies, Inc. 1757 West Adams St. Louis, MO 63122	*Central States Archeological Journal*
Oklahoma Anthropological Society 1000 Horn Street Muskogee, OK 74401	*Newsletter* and *Bulletin*
Oregon Archeological Society P.O. Box 13293 Portland, OR 97213	*Screenings*
Genuine Indian Relic Society, Inc. 3335 Junaluska Drive Columbus, GA 31907	*Prehistoric Art – Archaeology*
Northwest Arkansas Archeological Society, Inc. P.O. Box 1154 Fayetteville, AR 72701	*Arkansas Amateur*

XX. PROTECTION AND DISPLAY

Acquiring good points is very important but taking proper care of them is equally vital. The day when chipped Amerind art was tossed carelessly into a box is hopefully gone. And the practice of gluing and wiring points to a board damaged many specimens.

Point protection has several aspects. One is preventing damage through avoiding careless or unknowledgeable handling. Many fine points have been broken or chipped by dropping. Though flint is harder than a bare floor, points still break. Unprotected points are also subject to misplacement and theft.

For a collection of some value, security measures are in order, and finer pieces are sometimes kept in a home vault or bank safety deposit box. Some advanced collectors have an entire room that can be locked and is protect by electronic devices.

Weight-for-weight, some points are more valuable than gold, and prevention of loss is taken seriously. Some collectors take out insurance and an agent should be consulted for this step. Finally, a permanent photographic record should be made of all valuable points and the negatives stored in a safe place, not with the collection.

Display is a matter that ties in well with preventing loss or damage. Inexpensive black cardboard frames are available in several sizes and are the standard display-protection method used by many collectors. The white cotton or fabric backing cushions the points, holds them in position, and provides a good viewing contrast. Frames are also made of wood or metal and a list of frame suppliers ends this chapter.

Because of the relatively low cost, these frames are recommended for most collectors. Purchases in quantity substantially lowers the cost. Framed points can be displayed effectively and are easily handled, excellent for illustrating talks to groups and schools. This is an educational service that many collectors are more than willing to provide.

The author admits to a certain bias regarding how points are best arranged in a frame. Whether point or blade tips are "up" or "down" is a collector's decision and it depends on artifact and frame size. There is no one "correct" way.

The creation of figures with points, Indian profiles, and the like has largely passed from favor, as such pattern and designs tended to distract from the points themselves. Any placement in the frame that presents the points to best advantage is fine.

On this, here is worthwhile commentary from two gentlemen, both experienced point collectors, very active in the field. Gary Fogelman, editor/publisher of *Indian Artifact Magazine* (Box 240-RD #1, Turbotville, PA 17772) states "Most of my projectiles and scrapers are displayed on Riker mounts. If the frame contained an outstanding piece, either in workmanship or color, I tried to arrange the rest of the frame so that this would be evident.

"Something I have recently done is add color to the frames. Go to a hobby shop and obtain some $\frac{1}{16}$" or $\frac{1}{32}$" thick foam. You can then pad the entire frame with a color, as some artifacts show up better on colored foam than plain white. Black points go well with royal blue, green, and red and so do grey colors. White points look good on a rich red color and many other dark colors as well.

"Another thing I do is color code my collection. All material found on one site is given a color and so on. This gives a quick and easy method for picking frames from a certain site. Overall, let your imagination work for you."

Harvey E. King, collector and amateur archaeologist, and a member of the Oklahoma Anthropological Society since 1966, adds "Of prime importance to the collector are frames for mounting arrowheads, drills, scrapers, etc. Those with some carpentry skill, along with a few boards, 1" foam mattress topping, glue and nails can make their own frames.

"Seasoned collectors know the value of a well-catalogued collection. When numbering or printing on an artifact, select the least desired side, leaving the best or most perfect side uncluttered. Do very fine print. Old-timers used India ink, legible and permanent. An ultra-fine plastic-tip pen does a good job, so also a fine-tipped ballpoint pen.

"Your collection, well displayed, can create enormous interest, and give much personal satisfaction. Keep everything neat, clean, straightforward. Don't mix authentic pieces with replicas or fakes, or you will soon notice a lack of interest in your entire collection.

"Ben Thompson, 1757 W. Adams, Kirkwood, MO 63122, publishes the book *Who's Who in Indian Relics.* Hundreds of U.S. collectors are pictured with their displays. While the book serves as a record of collectors and their collections, many ideas for planning your own displays may be obtained from the photos."

Display Frame Suppliers:

Drabant's Antiques
P.O. Box 5268
Lincoln, NB 68505

Lenihan Associates
2130 Habberton Avenue
Park Ridge, IL 60068

Ground Floor Antique Shoppe
5722 Berry Lane
Little Suamico, WI 54141

Recaso Case Company
952 Sylvania Avenue
Toledo, OH 43612

Indian River Display Case Co.
13706 Robins Road
Westerville, OH 43081

Replica Products
610 - 57th Street
Vienna, WV 26105

These authentic points, averaging 2" long, have the insignia of earlier collectors on them, very difficult to interpret. They can be said to be "recollected" points, from unknown collections. The markings do not add to or detract from the pieces, each valued at $9.00-$15.00. (Lar Hothem Collection)

Heavy cardboard display/storage cases, small (6¾" x 8⅝") and large (12"x 16"), the last positioned face down. These display frames are ideal for most purposes and many collectors use them. (Lar Hothem photo)

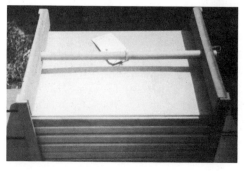

Ideal combinations for collectors, large wooden frames with glass fronts that fit into a handled frame carrier. This arrangement is excellent for both transportation and storage. (Lar Hothem photo)

XXI. ARROWHEADS AS ART

Most people, even non-collectors, know that Amerind points are artifacts. The word means mainly that they are objects shaped by human workmanship; the points were not created by elemental forces. But, are chipped points genuine art, worthy of the term, and worth time and money and popular recognition as works of art? The writer suggests that good points are good art, should be considered in that way, and collected in that way.

To be true art, any items should meet some general standards, prerequisites. They should be attempts to add to the work of nature and not unchanged acceptance of what was available. Indians did not throw whole great chunks of flint at food animals or enemies, but carefully shaped objects were thoughtfully made from that material, engineered to acceptable standards of the time.

A conscious effort must have been made to produce tools and points that not only worked well, but carried a sense of beauty. A high proportion of points evidence this, being nearly as useful today as scores of centuries ago. The points are still effective, and as an experiment, bowmen in recent years have actually hunted big game animals with them.

Beyond the beauty of continued usefulness is a clarity of perception. One knows, upon seeing an arrowhead, how it was used, what it was used for. Points were a form of art based on need. There was an added excellence in design, a high skill in execution. The pointmaker produced objects that are sought-after thousands of years later, no small accomplishment itself. One wonders that man-made objects today would compete with such an enviable record, or would even survive as long.

There is more evidence of points as prehistoric art, if only because so many seem to have been better made than they needed to have been. Great numbers were made from select materials, carefully chipped, extra-large. Why make a 6" point or blade when a 5" example would do?

Why choose a certain material, when a just as available, just as chippable but less attractive substance was at hand? Why make basal notching the same size, width, and depth when hafting corrections could have been produced a point just as useful? It would seem that the points were made to also please the maker.

Art can also be an advanced craft that uses proven steps to complete a desired product, the whole story of flint-knapping in North

America. From surviving examples, Amerinds in general mastered half a dozen flint-working techniques (see Chapter XIV). Each can be seen in various points, proving a skill level that is very easy to appreciate today.

None of us will ever have a conversation with a prehistoric pointmaker; questions of why this was done and not that will never be answered. The key inquiry, whether an artistic impulse was present at the time, will never be known.

What does matter is how artistic these forms are to us today. It should be noted that a whole range of points exists in all parts of the country, some of very poor materials and workstyle, that no one cares very much to investigate, name, or collect. These are the points that only have a "good personality" and sometimes not even that. Most collectors, upon encountering such a spiritless point, will dismiss it with "Well, it's probably not from around here."

Collectors with a serious interest in points realize that they are different from just being scientific statistics and are something more than curious Indian flints. The points themselves have a strange inner value that goes beyond pride of ownership or any monetary value.

Even the fact that fakers are turning out quantities of bogus points is a certain backhand compliment to the collecting field, in that it must be recognized as an art field. Probably these fakers, due to task concentration and skills in copying, should be termed "art forgers" and prosecuted as such.

An interesting aspect of points is that, except for ceremonial-grade pieces, they were made to be useful tools, not art objects. The makers may have considered themselves consummated technicians, in which case any pride would have been one of accomplishment, not creation.

Another thing that makes good points good art is the fact they were not made to be collected. (Although, there is proof that later peoples used the tools found from earlier groups. Even Indians collected arrowheads.) No maker could know that an alien race (us) would come from across the seas to inhabit the land, a people that would place high value on Amerind chipped tools.

The non-artistic aspect is that the makers never tried to produce for all time. The art aspect is that they managed it anyway.

In the whole range of points, there is always an inherent truth, a directness of purpose, a complex simplicity that has ageless appeal. All are parts of an art field. There is nothing, ever, of the self-conscious and blatant appeal of something purpose-made to be collected at a profit. No point was ever made to be of value for other than itself.

There is evidence that early people tried to create beauty for its own sake. The Archaic birdstone of the Midwest was pecked and polished from banded slate. They were sometimes made so that concentric banding in the head region formed an eye. A sense of artistry was indeed present, and there is no reason points would have been excluded from similar awareness. Often collectors comment that a point seems worked to show off the material and this happens so often it is far beyond happenstance.

A subtle, even subconscious part of the artistry of arrowheads is the people-to-people matter. Machines do not enter into this at all. The material was selected and transported to the chipping place by a human being. A human mind conceived the point form, hands chipped the piece, humans carried the point and used it and lost it. And now, this human touch is recognized for what it is, in what still exists, a mysterious awareness that crosses vast reaches of time.

On a more focused and personal level, points as art reach the heart and soul of the collector. An arrowhead seen in a field or arroyo, after all, is something one cannot *not* pick up. There is some sort of imme-diate attraction and attachment, something that cannot be explained. This emotional surge to acquire, or at least examine, is the basis for point collecting, and why it is unfathomable yet satisfying.

Good points as good art exhibit the skill and knowledge of the maker, and the more the maker knew, the better collectors appreciate the result. This goes beyond what must have been learned by example or repetition and approaches genius.

On the best of the best pieces, collectors sometimes just shake their heads, words being inadequate to express feelings. This finally would be the appropriate response for examining feelings. No better tribute could be given that maker, whose bones are now dust, but whose work will shine forever.

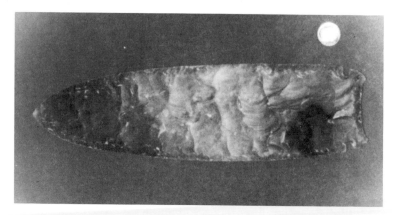

Caddoan blade, corner-notched, incurvate base. Of Edwards Plateau flint from Texas, this is one of the finest and longest (11¼") Caddo ceremonial blades ever found. It is AD 1250-1400 and from Arkansas. It is similar to the Gahagan style but a later variety with notches. Size, configuration, and delicate edge retouch make this one of the better North American flints and a true work of prehistoric art. Value: "Very valuable." (Sam and Nancy Johnson Collection, Arkansas)

Corner-tang knives, central Texas, in grey, tan, and black. Right blade 2½"; longest specimen 6". The heaviest concentration of these blades is in the Bell County area. Most of these blades are 4" to 5" long. The find ratio of other points to corner-tangs is 500:1. The blade type is ca. 1000 BC. These beautiful examples, fine condition, range in value from $200.00-$500.00 up to $1000.00 for blades over 6". Deliberately made to be asymmetrical, they are yet true works of chipped art. Specimen at top center may be considered classic. (Dwain Rogers Collection; Houston, Texas)

Desert side-notch 4⅜", lightly serrated edges, from Warner Valley, southeastern Oregon. Material is a light smoky obsidian that is translucent. When held to light, it reflects rainbow colors. Conclusive age is AD 1100-1200, but the type could go back many thousand years, possible to 10,000 BC. The words "balanced perfection" describe this artifact that most collectors would term a "gem-point's gem-point." Values approach the $1,000.00 range, depending on finder and buyer. Fine size and material in this piece; some collectors would place it in the $550.00-$1,000.00 range. Points or blades of this quality really have no upper value limitations. (Eugene Heflin Collection, Oregon)

Elko corner-notch point, expanding concave base, 1⅝" long. This example is of light amber-colored agate with transverse banding. This point has everything a collector looks for plus superb aesthetics in a gem material. Points of this ultra class can go as high as $1,500.00 and the comparatively small size is no drawback to appeal. (Eugene Heflin Collection, Oregon)

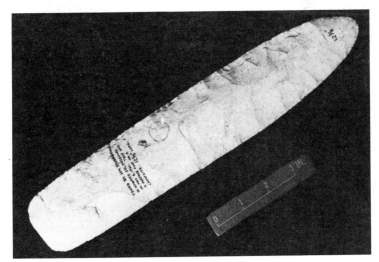

Wadlow blade, 12⅜" long, found in Howard County, Missouri in 1961 on a campsite. Large artifacts of this size and fine workstyle, in perfect condition, are increasingly rare and might well be classed as ceremonial. Of blue-grey material specimens, Wadlow blades are found in Illinois and Missouri and are late Archaic, ca. 1000 BC. Value: Museum grade. (Ben Thompson Collection; St. Louis, Missouri)

Gem-points, Columbia River area, many point and blade types, material and colors. Length is from ½"-4". Value range is as follows: Longest, $300.00-$800.00; mid-size, $50.00-$150.00; smallest, $15.00-$50.00. For pieces of this highest quality, there is no real or established top value, which máy vary. (Cliff Morris Collection, California; photo by Ray Pace, Associates)

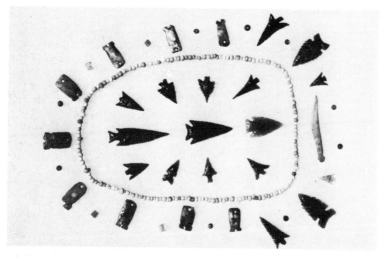

Art in obsidian: Columbia River gem-points, ¾"-3" long. (Abalone shell pendants from Santa Cruz Island, California; one hairpin from Santa Catalina Island, California; Mission beads, ca. AD 1600's, from Monterey, California.) The obsidian points and blades are among the finest produced in the Northwest and are outstanding in terms of size, balance, design, workstyle, etc. Values for smaller points, $50.00-$150.00 while longer blades are $350.00-$600.00. (Cliff Morris Collection, California; photo by Ray Pace, Associates)

Pedernales blades, 4¾"-5", Edwards Plateau flint, Comanche County, Texas. These specimens are outstanding is size, design, workstyle, and condition. Each is a top collector piece and each is in the $150.00-$300.00 range. (J.N. Thibault Collection, California)

Dovetails, longest example about 4". Left to right: Fractured base-corner dove, unusually wide notches, glassy flint, $200.00; Dovetail, classic shape, well-balanced, $250.00; Side-notch dove, wide base, delicate notching, $375.00; Notched-base dove, good base-center indentation, $550.00. (Private collection)

Blade, Plano-Paleo, just over 5" long. Material is a glossy blue and grey flint and the piece has unusual thinness at just over ¼" at centerline. Very delicate edge retouch adds to artistic impression and all dimensions are pleasingly balanced. It is hard to accept that a blade of this size and delicacy survived for 10,000 years. Values: $400.00-$500.00 and up. (Private collection, Ohio)

Dove-tail, in pale Flintridge chalcedony, about 4" long. Blades of this quality are extremely rare and are top collector pieces. $500.00 (BH Collection, Ohio)

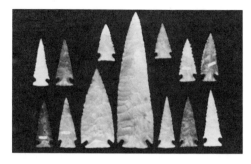

Ensor points and blades, 2½"-7", grey, white and tan. They are very well made. Ensors are $50.00-$300.00; large central blade, $900.00 (Dwain Rogers Collection; Houston, Texas)

Lost Lake basal-notched point just over 3". It is made of dark grey flint. Note basal grinding (edge smoothing) good balance in extended shoulders and excurvate line formed by base and both shoulder ends, ca. 4000 BC. Value: $450.00-$600.00. (Ben Thompson,Collection; St. Louis, Missouri)

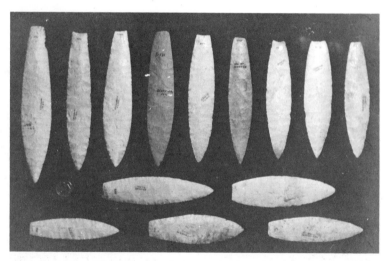

Beautiful grouping of superior grade Agate Basin points or blades, the longest specimen (far left) about 6". Agate Basin points are from ca. 7000 BC and are widely scattered finds in many Midwestern and Plains states, plus parts of lower Canada. Most are exceptionally well-chipped, with gently excurvate sides, slightly concave bases, and superb overall percussion and pressure flaking. Points of this size and quality are much-desired by collectors. Average value: $400.00-$900.00 each. (Ben Thompson Collection; St. Louis, Missouri)

Scottsbluff, 1¼" x 6¼", glossy flint, found near Agate Springs, Nebraska. This example is extremely well-flaked with basal edges ground and fine size, $800.00. (Kernaghan Collection, Colorado; Marguerite Kernaghan, photographer)

Rogue River points, gem quality. Left to right: Agate-point, barbed, $200.00; Agate-point, fine chipping, 1⅛", $450.00; Agate-point, $150.00 (Kernaghan Collection, Colorado; Stewart W. Kernaghan, photographer)

Dove-tail, eastern Midwest, a high-quality Archaic blade of creamy Flintridge material with high gloss. Condition, good size, form and workstyle combine to make a very superior piece. Blades of this caliber often sell for $500.00 or more. (Painter Creek Auction Service; Pandora, Ohio)

Marshall, 3", 3000 BC-AD 1000. White flint, very fine design and workstyle; note smoothness of excurvate edges, deep notching and exceptional shoulder-barbs, $300.00. (Arnold R. Logan Collection, Texas)

XXII. POINTS – What Are They Worth?

Point value can be a nebulous and touchy subject, for most collectors are first into points for love, and somewhere down the line, for money. It is rather like asking, "What are your children worth?" Point value is based partly on matters like a price originally paid, a perception of current fair market value and a personal preference and feelings.

One reluctance of collectors to state a value figure is a fear that this will be taken as an offer to sell, but communication can clear the air. Also, there is a definite attitude that it is low-class to mention money, but high-class to collect the pieces as art, even though money was paid. Some of the most admired points are those worth, at least potentially, a great deal of money. The whole thing on money sometimes is not so much the point, but who is selling and who is buying.

On value, there are factors of beauty that will always be true for the piece, but collector perception varies to an extent. If one doubts, there's this experiment that ought to take place more often. Say there is a point (there is one before me now) and it is fairly good, 2" long, no super qualities, no major drawbacks. The typical value is probably around $8.00.

Ask three collectors to rank it at $1.00-$5.00, $5.00-$15.00 and $15.00-$50.00, to value classify the point, and the three would probably place it in the second range where it likely belongs. But ask the hard second question, put a *precise* value on this point, and with no discussion or signals among the three people, agreement would be difficult.

One perceptive soul might say that the base is superior, the material satisfactory, so it's worth $7.00-$9.00, average $8.00. Another might note some mild edge wear and mark the point down to $6.00. The last member of the imaginary judging team might note that whatever our observations, the point is a fairly unusual type, fully worth $13.00, and is it for sale?

All would be close to market value, but all would see the same point from varied perspectives. But important here, the monetary values would not be joltingly different. It was not a dollar point, nor was it a $50.00 point. It was somewhere between $5.00 and $15.00. As one becomes aware of what points typically sell for, it is possible to narrow the range a great deal.

Relating to Chapter XV and Chapter XXI, the basic and the esoteric the question still remains as to real values. There are no established stock markets, no daily quotes. One cannot go to the supermarket and trade a point for food, unless the manager also happens to be a collector.

The standard psychology is pure buy-sell, the point being worth what it can be sold for. This cannot be argued, and probably a great number of points change hands at about what they are worth, neither being unusually high nor unusually low.

Two or more people, however, can bid at auction for a certain point or blade and drive the price far above that of an average collector. Sometimes there is an ego clash that pits towering collectors against one another, with a special point being sold at far above real worth. Several things happen.

The average collector may be driven from the market for that point class. The winning bidder may have spent $500.00 for what most would agree is a $300.00 point, the rest of the money being a sort of triumph over the other bidders. At times the worth of a point has some elements of maintaining a collector's self-image.

There are so many considerations as to what a point is worth that it is a topic that few know thoroughly. Does one look at size, type, material, workstyle, condition – or circumstance? If a point can help scientifically explain a certain aspect of a lifeway 5,000 years old, then its value is beyond reckoning or compare.

Price-wise, a point that is just another addition to a general collection doesn't "bring" much, for such pieces are more than common. They can often be replaced by better specimens at a similar cost, providing the buyer is somewhat selective.

A key point to complete a type collection – no matter the class – usually commands more money because the collector really wants it for reasons that go beyond the point itself. Just as a point somehow needs to be complete, so too do some collections, and it is a way of moving in a different direction or to another level.

Somewhat related is the matter of opportunity. If it has been awhile between major auctions or shows with good points, buyers may be "primed" to purchase. More collector dollars may be available, one reason why a major auction may be spread over a period of time.

Especially good weather may put purchasers in a buoyant mood, and bids are high. This usually does not mean a $10.00 point will sell for $40.00 or $50.00, but such touches can help explain why a $25.00 point sells for $35.00 or vice versa. Gift-buying is also an arena in which personal affection, or returning a favor, means that the item is more important than what was paid for it.

Economic press on the part of the seller can also shape point prices. I saw a frame of large blades for sale at a major outdoor flea market, offered at $225.00 from April through October. The 10 or 12 pieces had all signs of authenticity, no questionable attributes – yes, sometimes good points are offered at flea markets.

Several times I engaged in conversation with the seller about points in general, the frame in particular. It was felt that an average price of $20.00 per point was a bit high, that they were more (*average*, again) in the $15.00 category.

On the last day of the flea market, closing for the year, the writer made the standard admiring remarks. The seller, obviously disgusted with his inability to attract a buyer, abruptly offered the frame at less than half-price, cash. I countered with $95.00, plus $5.00 for the frame, and the offer was accepted. Under the right conditions, points can in fact be obtained at what must be near-cost, far below current market worth. The main factor in this bargain was a total lack of buyer competition.

Presentation is a way to enhance point value. A box of 20 good points with broken pieces thrown together never seems to reach the prices of those same 20 points mounted in an attractive frame. Like a museum artifact on a clear pedestal, or a jewel in a well-designed setting, the manner of display is very important. This adds to initial visual attraction and gives a favorable impression.

What an arrowhead or point is finally worth depends on the physical characteristics of it, type rarity, and buyer-seller situation, plus some psychological factors. The point is eventually worth the combination of these determinants.

Sooner or later, in these somewhat troubled economic times, the question comes up about investment value. Are good Amerind points a good and safe field for the future? The answer is, in general, "yes" but with some qualifications. This is hardly a get-rich-quick field, and collectors who buy foolishly (high prices for low-grade points) may have to wait for years to come out even. Needless to say, the purchase of a large number of fake pieces is simply a disaster.

It is true that old and authentic chipped pieces have never dropped greatly in value or shot up too wildly. This field is not fad market in which vague rumor (Dr. Acquisition's heirs are selling the collection) creates panic. Reflecting in a way the age of points, collecting them is a long-term matter and should not be approached with only profit in mind. The best collections are always put together with individual point quality first in mind, personal interest a close second, and the price tag a distant third.

A collector would be well-advised to put satisfaction and overall enjoyment ahead of any future monetary considerations. This is, or should be, the guideline for any collection. Otherwise, it is only another disguised form of money-making activity or work. The sincere point collector with good judgment and some available money will not be funding a losing proposition, for excellence will always be recognized.

The money angle, whether a present purchase or future value of the collection must be answered with the cryptic remark, "It depends." It depends in large part on how much the collector knows, how much he or she learns through study and intuition and other personal efforts. Hopefully, as a most worthwhile gift to the point collector, this book will suggest far more questions than answers.

XXII. ADVICE TO COLLECTORS

This chapter deals with some distilled wisdom about the collecting of prehistoric Indian projectile points and blades. The information has been taken from many sources and is presented here in a series of self-contained paragraphs.

For a beginner acquiring the first points, it would be well to have an experienced friend on the first trip or two. Remember, a less-than-perfect, or fake, point is almost impossible to get rid of. If you collect it, you are likely stuck with it.

With agricultural lands being taken out for other projects and "no-till" (non-plowing) farming gaining favor due to reduced costs and decreased soil erosion, fewer points are being found each year. One thing that has kept point prices somewhat reasonable has been this resupply factor. This is now changing and values will soon reflect a growing shortage of newly found points.

Collect the best points you can afford and only sell them if the collection is being upgraded. The attraction of point collecting is usually so deep that those who let collections go, for whatever reason, are usually sorry later. The *meaning* of it is somehow greater than the sum of the parts.

Know the "keys" to what you collect. For instance, other artistic/value aspects aside, the key to fluted points is the flute. Depending on regional type, the actual fluting should be distinctive, not come too close to lower side edges, be medium deep, and perhaps end in the peculiar marks called hinge fractures, a tiny stairstep up to the face surface. Two flutes (one each side) are better than one only on one side, and they should be of about equal length and width. Multiple fluting should be of similar widths and lengths, harmonious to the piece.

Purchase as many good books as you can, pertaining to artifacts, their manufacture, age, use, etc. Take every advantage to visit with advanced collectors. Most will be delighted to show their collection, talk about points, and offer helpful tips. Instead of ignoring fakes, learn all you can about them.

Leave a will legally stating exactly what happens to your collection. If it is as important as you feel it is, put this importance on paper.

When visiting a collector, don't pick up or touch points unless it is understood to be permitted. Do praise (if you wish) points that are obviously fine and hold back comments on what are not. Don't be quick to term a piece "fake" even if you think it is. This can be a serious insult to the collector, who might believe it to be good. If the collector personally found the point, then your judgment is in question.

The word "fake" is itself now an emotional issue and circumstances dictate a careful use of the term. A point is indeed fake if it is modern-made and knowingly presented as authentic. It is a reproduction if it is offered as modern-made. It is a replica if a copy or cast of an authentic piece, used for display, teaching, etc. It is a partial fake if a restored point is knowingly offered as an entirely original piece.

For a truly good point collection, don't acquire objects other than points. Then, a point accumulation will suffer because of diluted effort. Emphasis or focus is everything.

When viewing a private collection, unless the owner is stressing point values, don't concentrate on what any one point is worth. Many collectors do not keep up on values, and this is only one aspect (often a minor one, or the least important) of worth to the owner. A person interested only in point values misses the essence of point collecting.

Whenever possible — and the points are good, the asking figure reasonable — purchase entire collections. Good information on point origins is generally available, and per-item cost is often much less than if points are obtained piece-by-piece.

If welcomed to view another's collection, it is his or her hour or two. If you want to be invited back, don't interrupt every few minutes with comments like, "Nice, but I have one just like it, only an inch longer and of better material." Forget "oneupsmanship" and be both generous and fair.

As time passes and the collection grows, it is easy to forget where individual points came from. Dates and places slip away. Cataloging every point in the collection is a must. A fine collection is classified as such when the history of each item displayed is recorded. Use your own system, keep it consistent, and updated.

Large artifact shows, such as those held in the states adjoining the Mississippi River Valley, are a good place to collect points. Whatever you want, you can find there. Hundreds of collectors and dealers attend, points can be inspected, and the presentation for sale of fake points is prohibited.

When talking about points, be honest with information. If you know about a point type, fine. If you don't, say so. Some collectors are known by certain derogatory names because (so it seems) the less they know, the more they expound. Some very knowledgeable people in the field spend most of the time listening.

Integrity and reputation are synonymous in the point-collecting field because such a large part of interaction is based on trust. Probably more than in any other collecting area, word very quickly gets around if shady practices are employed. Once a reputation for honesty and fairness is faded, one may as well begin collecting cobwebs.

Often, in point collecting, it is not so much how much you have, but what you know about what you have. A quality collection, in short, is the by-product of the quality of the collector's knowledge.

XXIV. UNCHIPPED POINTS

It would be misleading to leave an impression that all Amerind points were chipped from quartz-family materials. Such is not the case at all. A variety of substances was used, and points were shaped in other ways. While the number of non-chipped points is relatively small compared with chipped objects, these points are yet an important addition to the weapons inventory of early North American inhabitants.

Bone was very widely used and some experts even believe that there were pre-lithic (before *Clovis* and *Sandia* points) peoples over 20,000 years ago. It may well be that, if so, their toolkit was made of shaped bone artifacts. Dates from Old Crow Flats sites in Canada in fact suggest a time frame of plus-25,000 years of age.

To make bone points, large bones were split with heavy hammers, and the sharp pieces were cut into shape, then ground and polished against loose-grained stones. Often the bone (as with the Eastern Sioux) was worked flat and inserted in the projectile tip like any other point. A few bone points were made to resemble flint types, but most had special shapes, if only long and pin-like. This all brings up the thought of animal species being hunted with points made from their own kind.

Horn and antler were also favorite materials, with the added advantage of some parts being already sharp-tipped. Deer antler was often used in the Midwest, and wherever the white-tailed deer flourished, which was most of the Continental U.S. Most antler-tine points were several inches long, straightened somewhat by abrasion, and had a hollow-socket base for the projectile shaft. A few points had a long, angled shoulder to act as a barb. Ground and polished elk horn was used in northern California and elsewhere.

Wooden points were a natural extension of wood shafts and fire-hardened points were probably fairly common. Wood points – being organic, as are bone and antler – did not survive the centuries well and most have disappeared. Wood points ranged from a simple sharpened tip to larger points which were also one-piece with the shaft.

Ivory, often combined with bone or wood, was used in the Pacific Northwest, especially on the Bering Coast. A common form was the unique point known as a harpoon with barbed and detachable head. This was secured to a strong line so that struck prey could be retrieved. Fish and sea mammals of many kinds and sizes were taken in this manner, and the harpoon was used in much of North America.

Iron and steel points were used in historic times after the Indians recognized the value of the new metal. In early historic or Contact times,

Amerind hunters obtained metal for arrowheads from such sources as barrel hoops, wheel rims and broken iron kettles. Even brass was occasionally worked, if a supply source could be found, such as discarded utensils.

Later, the all-purpose iron trade was made by Whites for Amerinds use. The basic form was a long, very thin triangular point with a narrow stem which had dull serrations for shaft-binding. These are interesting (and valued at $6.00 to $12.00 each, depending on size and condition) if only because they were the Whites' idea of what an Indian arrowhead should be.

Some North American Indians had their own metal age. Copper was used extensively in the Upper Midwest, in Michigan, Wisconsin and Lower Canada. The yellow-gold metal was not melted or poured into forms, but pure nuggets were pounded into shape.

The Old Copper Culture (5000-3000 BC) of the eastern Upper Midwest used copper for several thousand years, and countless points were made. There is some evidence that copper was heated to make the pounding-out process easier, but the temperature does not seem to have reached the smelting level.

While the Old Copper people made many other types of artifacts from copper, perhaps their projectile points, lanceheads, show the most style diversity. At least seven different point basal configurations were made of the following types: long and tapered ("rat-tail" to collectors), partial wrap-around, straight-stem, expanded-stem, contracted-stem, serrated-stem, and hollow-socket base.

With all this, the Old Copper artisans also fashioned a number of flint point types. This suggests the constant value and utility of chipped points, even when another material was easily available. Compared with flint, obsidian and the many other chipped artifacts, unchipped points for one reason or another are scarce today. Regional collectors like to specialize them when such points can be found.

Iron points and blade, largest piece 1⅛" x 3¾", all flound with metal detector near Ft. Leavenworth, Kansas. Long thin point, lower right, was made from a nail file. Values: $20.00-$35.00, center blade, $60.00. (Kernaghan Collection, Colorado; Marguerite Kernaghan, photographer)

Steel points and blades, trade goods, early historic, made from old knives. Longest piece is 1" x 5½". Smallest was surface find near Agate Springs, Nebraska. Values from $35.00-$90.00. (Kernaghan Collection, Colorado; Marguerite Kernaghan, photographer)

Metal points, historic, various regions, largest piece 2⅛" long. Middle left: New Mexico; middle right, Nebraska; bottom right, New Mexico; top left, Colorado; all others Pennsylvania. These trade or Indian-made points are valued from $12.00-$50.00 with size, lines and condition important factors. (Kernaghan Collection, Colorado; Marguerite Kernaghan, photographer)

Copper points, largest ¾" x 1⅝", from shore of Lake Michigan. All have good patina. Values: $12.00-$35.00 each. (Kernaghan Collection, Colorado; Marguerite Kernaghan, photographer)

GLOSSARY
Projectile Point Terms

Agate (point): Term that describes small points of super-fine material, mainly used in Western U.S. The actual material is a variety of chalcedony with banded colors or irregular clouding.

Archaic (point): Projectile point or blade from the prehistoric hunting/gathering lifeway. Dates for the period differ across the country, but most are in the BC period.

Arrowhead: Broad term that commonly refers to all chipped Amerind artifacts with tip and base. True arrowheads are late prehistoric, most after AD 500 and were bow-propelled.

Asymmetrical: Unbalanced point outline, viewed at either face, i.e., left and right parts are dissimilar. Some blades, like the SW corner-tang blades, were deliberately made asymmetrical in form.

Authentic: An "honest" point or feature of it, all being old and original; the opposite of a fake piece.

Barbs: Usually features of a stemmed point, these are sharply back-tapered shoulder tips that offer a barbed configuration. In a few cases, barbs may be on point sides.

Basal smoothing: Base edge dulling, frequently done in the Paleo and Archaic time frames, by rubbing chipped edges against a softer stone. This helped prevent hafting thongs from being cut when in use.

Basal thinning: Chipping basal material from both lower faces to thin the point and make it easier to attach. This was done with many point types.

Base: Bottom or hafting area of point or blade.

Base-notched: Indentations for binding are located somewhere in the point bottom, ranging from near center to near edges.

Bevel (edge): The word "bevel" is often used to mean the whole point or blade type that has beveled or angled edges. The edge itself is sharply canted to one side, chisel-like in profile which can be quickly resharpened and gives great strength.

Bi-edged shaper: Artifact made from broken point bases, the break area ground to form a working area on edges along each face side. From all time periods, these may have been used to shape lanceshafts, etc.

Bifurcate: Word refers to point or blades with bifurcated bases. The base projection is divided into two separate lobes, with a notch-like space between. Many bifurcates have bases that could almost be considered tri-notched.

Birdpoint: Old term for small late-prehistoric arrowheads, generally less than ¾" long. It was once thought they were used to shoot birds, but current thought is that they are general-purpose arrowheads.

Blade: Overall word that indicates a knife form, a chipped artifact that was probably used for cutting. Some types, however, seem also to have been used as projectile points.

Bladelet: Small knife, generally one that is long and thin, struck from the parent core with one blow. Here, chipping dynamics resemble flute-removal from certain Paleo point bases.

Blank: Finished artifact, except that basal notching or stemming (and perhaps edge retouching) have not been completed. (See also "preform")

Blunt: Several meanings. It can mean a point without a fine tip, but more often, a point that terminates part way up the face. The area is rechipped in a straight or excurvate edge. It was once thought these were small-game "stunners" but most show signs of having been used as scrapers.

Broken: Incomplete point, especially major damage.

Cache (blade)**:** Certain types of knives or large points often found in numbers as underground deposit. They range from nondescript performs or blanks to such types as the Turkey-tail and all time periods can be represented.

Calcium deposit: Whitish to grey adherents often found on artifacts recovered from limestone dry caves and rock shelters.

Ceremonial: Any point or blade that does not seem to have been made from actual use. The ceremonial aspect may be indicated by extra-large size, super-fine workstyle and rare materials or purposeful dulling of working edges.

Color: Points of spectacular material, standouts because of attractive hues.

Core: The "parent" material from which long flakes or bladelets are struck.

Corner-notched: Notches put into shoulder-end area, leaving the basal area largely untouched.

Damage: Missing point portions, generally less severe than breaks, which often produce flaws in the point outline. Damage can either have been done in prehistoric or more recent times.

Dealer: One who buys and sells (and often collects) points.

Downgrading: Negative comments about an artifact, often at auction previews, to attempt to lessen later bidding competition.

Duo-notched: Unusual points with a double set of notches, usually in a stem-like base, sometimes on lower point sides.

Dull (material): Point surfaces that do not reflect light well; non-glossy.

Ears: Base ends that extend out beyond the sides of point or blade.

Eccentrics: Small chipped objects that do not seem to have any purpose. Though many specimens are not authentic, some prehistoric specimens have been found. Their purpose is unknown.

Edge wear: Slight to heavy edge dulling of a blade, caused by normal prehistoric use.

Equipment strike: Damage done to a field-found point by agricultural equipment. This may range from mild edge-chipping to major and complete breakage.

Ex. coll.: A point that is known for certain to have once been in a (usually well-known) collection.

Exotic: Not of the region. An exotic point may be so-called because of out-of-area form, material, or both.

Face: The wide sides of a point, the area between tip and base.

Fake: Modern or recently chipped specimen, often made to resemble prehistoric types. A fake becomes fraudulent if it is knowingly represented as authentic.

Flakes: Bits of flint or obsidian chipped away in point manufacturing.

Flake scars: Point indentations from which chips were removed.

Flute: Long, thin channels chipped from the lower faces of certain Paleo-period points, extending from base toward tip.

Fracture chipping: A specialized chipping technique done in the basal area on some nearly finished points; a thin sliver of material was removed from edges. Apparently, this was a short-cut edge dulling method. Hence, a "fractured" point may still be in perfect condition.

Gempoint: A well-made point of ultra-fine material. The term is sometimes used for certain NW Coast specimens, but is also applied elsewhere. The words "gem quality" are also used.

Glossy: Surface sheen of a point, due to reflected light. Generally, the higher the gloss, the better the material quality.

Grave deposit: Organic deposits of various kinds sometimes found on points associated with graves.

Grinding: Base-area grinding done to point in prehistoric times to dull edges in hafting area.

Haft: The part of a point or blade that was fastened to shaft or handle.

"Heartbreaker": Collector term for a superb surface found point or blade, but in broken or damaged condition.

Heat-treated: Material that may have been fire-altered in prehistoric times as a preparation step for chipping.

Knife: Blades that were used with a short handle for general or specialized puncturing or cutting tasks. Many large and intermediate "points" were probably used as knives.

Lancehead: Projectile point once fitted to a light javelin and propelled by a hand-held wooden launcher, the *Atl-atl.*

Lanceolate: Lance-like, a configuration that is long, narrow, rather dagger-like, with slight if any shouldering. The term is often used for late-Paleo points or blades.

"Lightning" lines: Streaks or thin veins of light or translucent material that meander through darker point material.

Lobes: Lower extensions of the point base center, especially the large, round bifurcate area.

Local material: Points made of a chipping substance that existed nearby, generally easily identifiable.

Maltreatment: Certain indignities suffered by points after being found. This includes damage of any kind caused by careless handling, etc.

Marked: Provenance data on certain points, often black Indian ink on light material, white ink on dark. Notations may include date found, place/locality, and name of the finder. Older examples are increasingly scarce and may be considered "signed."

Mounting chips: Small opposing indentations on points that were once wired to frame sheets for display purposes.

Museum quality: General term denoting highest and best point types and grades.

Named: Points with enough distinctive features to be given an identifying "class" name. Most such points exist in fairly large numbers.

Notches: Rounded or oblong indentations chipped from the base for hafting purposes.

Old breaking: Any damage actually done in prehistoric times.

Paleo: Points and artifacts from early hunting times, usually 8000 BC and earlier.

Patina: Surface discoloration or deposits as a result of age, weathering and earth chemicals. Basically, patina is how the exterior of a point differs from the interior.

Percussion flaking: Chipping method that employed blows from bone or antler tools to remove fairly large face and edge chips; sometimes punch-and-hammer tools were used.

Perfect: A point without breaks or damage and exactly as the Amerind artisan made it.

Point: Common term for projectile points. A point's point is the tip.

Potlid: Small conical pits in a point or fragment that prove it was once in a fire. Tiny amounts of water were turned to steam, blowing out a section of material.

Preform: Any early stage of point manufacture, often somewhat rough, with few type identifying characteristics.

Prehistoric salvage: The reworking of points into other tools or weapons. Many points thus became hafted scrapers, bi-edged shapers, even drills.

Pressure flaking: Chipping done with tools directed by hand and finger pressure. Often the more delicate chipping was done in this manner.

Projectile point: Any point that was probably mounted as a lancehead or arrowhead.

Provenance (also **provenience**): Point origin or source; the historic record of a point. This is certain proof of where a point has been since it was found.

Questionable: A point that does not appear to be totally authentic or totally fake, but has attributes of each. Most collectors do not seek to acquire such pieces.

Recent damage: Point chippage or breakage done either by agricultural equipment, by finder or by owner.

Reproduction: The recreating of points using prehistoric chipping techniques, done as an exercise in knowledge or skill. If not represented as old or authentic, reproduction points are not technically fake or fraudulent.

Resharpened: Edge rechipping of a blade or point to enhance effectiveness, done long ago.

Restoration: Reforming the missing part(s) of a point using materials that eventually resemble that of the original.

Rework: Any rechipping done in prehistoric times to continue point or blade effectiveness. The word can also mean modern chipping done to remove signs of damage.

Serrations: "Sawtooth" blade or point edges to improve penetration or cutting ability.

Shaman's piece: Chipped object with peculiar man-made wear or heavy polish, of no known use or meaning.

Shoulders: Lower sides and ends of a point.

Side-notched: Hafting notches that are somewhere on the point sides, nearer the base than tip.

Single-notch: Hafting notch, usually proportionately large, at the center of the base bottom.

Solution cavity: Indentations or holes left in a point when softer material has eroded away.

Spearpoint: Common term for large chipped point-like artifacts. Most such specimens were probably knives.

Stain: Discoloration of a point or part(s) due to soil conditions, grave association or farming chemicals.

Stem: Protruding point basal column, used for hafting purposes.

Surface find: Point picked up in agricultural or non-tilled terrain, found on top of the earth.

Symmetrical: "Balanced" point with left and right sides very similar.

Tip: The top end of a point or blade.

Translucent: Material, generally of very high quality, that permits the passage of some light.

Triangular: Point outline with long sides and straight or incurvate baseline. Many late-prehistoric arrowheads are of such of configuration.

Tri-notch: Point with three notches, usually two on opposite lower sides and one in base center.

Type point: Chipped artifact that is easily identifiable with many others of similar design.

Variation: A point with some type attributes but with minor differences; major differences might indicate a sub-type.

Warpoint: Old term for simple unnotched triangular arrowheads, in the belief that projecting shoulders made the points stay in a wound. These are probably late-prehistoric general-purpose arrowheads.

Water-worn: Projectile points, especially early types, that have been abraded and polished by wave/sand action. Such finds are made on lakeshore and ocean beach sites.

Schroeder's
ANTIQUES
Price Guide

. . . is the #1 best-selling
antiques & collectibles value guide on the market today,
and here's why . . .

• More than 300 advisors, well-
known dealers, and top-notch collectors work together with our editors
~~~~~ ccurate information
and identification.

45,000 items in
~~ories are listed
of sharp origi-
e not only the
the common,
well.

shot shows
y. Every sub-
histories and
on, a feature
r competitors'

abreast of
rends, often
categories a

'll find it in
n we publish
k each cate-
ely reflective
y the best of

Sch
is u
gor
of r
the

R BOOKS
Publishing Co., Inc.

reliable information and values.